LIVING IN TWO WORLDS

MY JOURNEY

Karen Kelsall

LIVING IN TWO WORLDS

ISBN: 9798629546344

Website: kazkelsall.webs.com/never forever

LIVING IN TWO WORLDS

Acknowledgements

I would like to thank my soul mate Steve who keeps me on my toes, my loving daughter Natalie for always believing in me, my sister Maria who is a lovely soul, my step children Beth and Sam who should go grab the world with both hands, and my loving Grandchildren Sydney Rae, Freya Jade and Max James who I know will go far in this world. Carol Fowke and Jackie Hollis, I could not do what I have done with my life without you both, to my spiritual sisters Pat Wood and Dawn Shury, and to all my friends who have been with me through the good and bad times along my spiritual path, I bless you.

To all those who have passed, my son, my brother Stephen, Nan and Grandad. To everyone I have mentioned in this book and last but not least those whose spirits came through to me when they were needed.

Contents

1. In The Beginning

When I was a child, I always felt that I was different, I felt awkward, and that I did not belong to my family.

I suppose it may have all started before I was born. My Mother was eight and a half months pregnant with me and was verbally and physically attacked by a stranger whilst walking in the street, my Mother's attacker claimed that she was his wife. My Mother made her way back to her home in a state of shock and the incident brought about early labour. My Mother had to ask a passer-by to find the nearest phone box and call for an ambulance.

My mother was taken to hospital, which was a very sparse and old Canadian Air Force barracks. Labour progressed quickly and I was delivered in the hospital bed whilst the nurses were in their office listening to the radio. What an entrance that was as the nurses had to take me from under the covers of her bed!

Strange thing was when I was a child I used to end up sleeping through the night with my head under the covers at the bottom of the bed. Some things you don't grow out of!

I lived with my Grandparents from birth, my sister lived with my parents as financially things were tough. I was apparently a restless baby and would not settle for my Grandmother unlike my older sister who was angelic and slept well and was blessed with a sunny disposition.

My parents lived in a flat and from time to time, I stayed with them and then went back to my Grandparents' house, this went on for about the first five years of my life. My Grandparents' house was old and had 'visitors' living there too which I came across at an early age. I was told years later that my nappies and milk bottles for baby formula used to be thrown across the room and a lot of banging noises and bad smells emanated from parts of the house. One of the 'visitors' made it clear that they were not used to a baby being in the house. My nan was calm about the poltergeist activity in her house and I remember vividly of her telling "someone" off when it got too much for all of us in the house. She was not scared of the spirits and if she was, she didn't show it. I feel this is where I learnt to react calmly to my future incidents of spirit visitations.

My first actual sighting of a 'ghost' was when I was around three years old. I clearly remember this as if it was yesterday. I was coming out of the front room to go into the hall, and as I looked up the stairs there was a man in a dark haze, not completely a silhouette, standing on the stairs looking at me. I shouted for my nan to come to me and as I pointed to the man and told her about him, she said there was no man on the stairs, yet I could see him as plain as day. She calmly said again that there was no man there. I was so confused and didn't want to say it again as my nan was a strong but fair lady and you didn't need to be told twice, if the answer was no then it is NO!

As I got older, she told me there were people in the house and was more open about it when things started to happen in front of me.

After that incident, I used to see him more on the landing especially in the evening. As I went up the stairs, I would then feel an uneasy feeling in my stomach about what was on the landing, knowing the visitors on the landing were waiting for me. I used to walk sideways with my back against the bannister to reach my bedroom. One visitor was a strong, dark energy who used to stand against the opposite wall but there was also another energy who kept the dark energy at bay, protecting me. I tried to avoid going near the blackness on the landing as it really scared me as I wasn't sure what it was.

There was a lot of activity which was assumed as normal because I was too young to understand. My Nan used to talk to the visitors and that was because she could see and speak to spirit. This went on for a few years.

My Uncle lived in my Nan and Grandad's house too so with a child being in the house as well it must have been strange for them. We all had to wash in the kitchen sink, at separate times of course and use the tin bath on certain days. There was no bathroom and the toilet was in a little shed at the bottom of the yard at the back of the house. That was an experience in itself!
If I didn't go to the toilet before I went to bed, then woe betide me. I would not want to go in the yard in the middle of the night, so I would hang on until the morning. Visiting before bedtime, in the dark, being thankful if the light bulb worked, and greeted by the biggest garden spider you would ever see. There was a nail in the wall for the toilet roll or sheets of cut up

newspaper if we had run out. I would have one eye on the spiders and one eye on the door in case it blew open.

My imagination ran wild in that toilet as it verged on to the communal path to the neighbours. Being three years old, I had to reach to pull the chain, turn the light off and run my little legs back to the house. I have fond memories of that house, we didn't have much, but we did have laughter.

I was about five when I went back to living with my parents at their house, which again had a different energy. I was introduced to my baby Brother and my older Sister who I had been seeing over the years. The atmosphere in our family was difficult due to my Brother having been born with learning difficulties and the tension created between my parents affected my Sister and I.

Living at home with my family was different to living with my grandparents. My sister and I were different people, we were not alike. Chalk and cheese, we were called. When she was little, she showed me a lot of affection, but I was untouchable. I remember saying to my mother that this is not my family and I do not belong here. I could not stand public displays of affection and I was quite isolated as I did not belong with them. I was not sure at that time if I was missing my life with my grandparents or if I felt I actually had memories of living with another family in a past life.

I used to say to them, 'You are not my mother and you are not my sister'. This was a regular occurrence for me to feel this way. I would look at my family and think what am I doing here and where is my other family. My mother couldn't understand my outbursts and frustration. I was not relating to my family at all. Talk of me seeing ghosts or any weird events happening to me were forbidden.

At the age of about seven, whilst living with my family, I started to see a man in a black suit and top hat on the top of the stairs near the landing. What is it with men on the landing I do not know! He was there in the daytime and night-time. Many times I would come out of the toilet and be greeted by him standing there. I would turn the landing light off and run into my bedroom and I would see my sister (we shared the bedroom), looking at me and wondering why I looked worried. It dawned on me that she could not see him.

I used to doodle weird pictures in my books. I remember one in particular was a hand with an eye in the palm and also geometric patterns of a sky at night. I used to dream of a different place, where I was living in a different country as if I was recalling memories. As I grew older, I became aware that I was seeing things other children and adults could not.

At my grandparents' house I came across a spirit called Mr Parks. My nan spoke to him and called him that name. It was only when I was much older that she explained to me who Mr Parks was, and why he was in the house. The story was that in his own house many years before, one of his daughter's was promised by her fiancé that when he returned from the war, he would marry her. What transpired was that when he came back from the war, he called off the engagement with her and he married her sister instead. The sorrow she had was so great. One day Mr Parks found out the hard way how it had affected her.

Mr Parks came home to be told that his daughter in her sorrow had hung herself in her bedroom. She could not take the rejection and then saw her sister marrying him. In his anguish, Mr Parks had decided to brick up the doorway of her bedroom as he could not face going in there. He and his family left the house but left some furniture behind, and this is where my nan and grandad and seven children moved in and lived there for some years.

I was told that the energy was strong in that house and everyone felt it. When my grandparents' and their children left the house, they took the furniture from the house to their new house as they had no money for new furniture. This was to prove to be a bad decision.

The furniture was key to bringing the negative energy into the new house. The energy was Mr Parks and the negative energy of something else that may have been attracted to the sorrow and death of his daughter. The two energies were present in the house for years. When he was around you certainly felt him. He used to walk around the house every day and you would hear and see the living room door being pushed open and these were very hard, heavy doors to open.

Mr Parks used to walk behind the settee you were sitting on. On the back of your neck you would feel a cold static feeling behind you before he walked across the room to the other door to go into the kitchen. This came to be a normal occurrence. My nan used to say hello to him as he was walking across the room and glanced over in his direction.

I believe he was the good energy that was keeping the other energy at bay. Things used to disappear and then later appear when my nan told the spirits to return it. She spoke to them with such ease but was firm when needed to be.

LIVING IN TWO WORLDS

2. *Things Are Happening*

Back at my family's house I was now getting used to being different. At the age of eight, I was deemed as partially deaf as my hearing had got worse. My mother used to take me to the Birmingham Clinic for the Deaf. These were regular visits to a doctor who would probe in my ears. The one thing that I can still remember, was thinking it was a bit unusual for a doctor to heat a metal pincer over an open flame and then putting it in my ears, to open up my narrow ear canals. It hurt a little and this was done with no words spoken, not that I would hear them. Every time the doctor at the clinic put the hot metal pincer in my ears, I then had a hearing test in an insulated room, which meant wearing headphones and to try and hear all different tones of noises from a machine in another room, that they sent to my headphones. Some were vibratory, some were hissing and also high- & low-pitched tones. If I heard a tone then I was to tap the table with a ruler and through the window outside the room where they were sending the noise to me, they would watch me, and I assume take notes. This was done over three years through junior school.

I would have ear drops in my ears four times a day which

meant coming home at dinner time to have it done and go back to school afterwards. My mother administered this every day. It must have been a chore to her and was a pain to me, but it was to help. My parents got quite frustrated with the situation especially my father as he used to shout at me when I did not hear what he had told me to do etc. I could read his lips and then I knew he was angry. One night it came to a head and because I could not hear him, he shouted at me and my mother said, 'You know she cannot hear' so he then called me 'Cloth-Ears', which is a description in itself. I heard or should I say lip read that a lot.

I am not sure if they knew I could lip read but to me that was one way for me to communicate and not feel alone in silence. One day I started to hear muffled sounds and after one visit to the Deaf Clinic, I told them I could hear the sounds in the headphones. The doctor there must have thought 'Right let's go for it', so he put the hot pincer in my ears again and then sat back and looked at me. He then started to speak to me, and I could hear him talk. I was so shocked as it had been a very long time since I had heard anything.

My mother was with me when we left the clinic that day and as soon as we walked out onto the busy street, the first thing I heard was traffic and it was very noisy too. I remember putting my hands to my ears and yelping, thinking that is loud. We got home by bus and that was weird hearing people talking in different voices. The one thing which sticks in my mind for loudness was when I went to the toilet. I flushed the toilet and I remember running out as it was so loud and told my mother it scared me. After all that time not hearing my family talking, it was a really different and new experience for me. Sometimes I wished I could shut it all out again but saying that I did not want to be deaf again.

At the age of eight I started to notice in my dreams, I could see light coming from my hands and fingertips. One day a watch I used to wear stopped working, being a wind up watch I forwarded the time on it, yet it would stop working. My mum could not understand it and gave me another watch, that worked for a few minutes and that stopped too. Some watches went faster and were way ahead of the time. She thought I had put them on something magnetic like the fridge, but I hadn't. I still cannot wear watches. I have to put them in my handbag.
I became more magnetic. Sparks came from my hands if I touched metal door handles, sometimes shocks were given to people when I touched them. If my mum thought I was a weird child then, she was not far wrong.

My dreams were taking a turn for the adventurous. I would lie in bed and feel myself start to rise off my bed. Just as I was dropping off to sleep, I would hear a buzzing sound or humming sound and then start to float above my bed, at will sometimes. I would escape in my dreams and go to places I have never seen before. When I was older, I learnt that I was actually Astral Travelling and was to continue to do this many years later.

The strangest one I recall was when I was nine years old. I was wearing my nightdress and I then started to rise from my bed. I looked down to see my sister fast asleep. I then floated out of the bedroom window, and started to float in the night air, over my garden and continued down the back roads until I reached my friend's house who lived a few roads away. It seemed so easy for me to go through the brick wall of her house. I was aware that everyone was asleep as it was late at night. I stood on the landing and my friend's mother came out of her bedroom and walked past me to go to her bathroom. I was alarmed as she did not see me. I then went back out of her house and floated back to my bedroom and landed on my bed with a thud and I awoke startled.

The next day at school, I told my friend that I had seen her Mother last night and described my dream and the nightwear her mother was wearing. I had never been upstairs in her house before, yet I could tell which bedroom was her parents. She thought it was magical and she told her parents. This was to be the last time I went in her house as her parents didn't see the magical side of it. Her mother rang my mum and said that I was not to come to her house again. She was worried about her daughter's friendship with me as I was a little different. It seemed I described her nightwear accurately and told my mother so.

I also started to have premonitions. I would know when something was going to happen or I dreamt it in a film 'like image' and for days or a while later, the event would show itself as I saw it. I knew when people were not well, or something was troubling them as I would feel their energy.

I was a sickly child and if I was near someone in a shop or in their home, I would pick up their illness or emotional state. I still feel this now, but I am aware of it and have to protect myself. It is called being an empathic person.

It was hard being different as none of my friends nor family understood me and it certainly wasn't talked about. My nan confided in me one day that she knew I saw spirit and did not want to frighten me by telling me when I was so young. She also said my mum saw spirit sometimes but chose not to accept it and she kept her premonitions a secret too.

Things were hard at home with my parents, the tension in the house was bad, you were walking on eggshells. Not knowing if not putting the milk bottles outside or doing a chore wrongly would mean the usual punishment. My parents were strict disciplinarians and had a way with dealing with things that others may not have reacted to. I am now aware that they were treated in that manner too so only thought it was normal parenting.

The problem was that it had got too much for myself and my siblings. My brother was a nervous child who wet the bed until he was about eight years old. I had to wake him up late in the evening and during the night to take him to the toilet, as he would sleep heavily and wet the bed not knowing, but he still had accidents.

I am not sure if he had the 'influence' as people would call someone with psychic gifts. A few times I would go to his bedroom to wake him up for the usual walk to the toilet and he would be sitting bolt upright staring out ahead, as if he was looking at someone or something. Sometimes he used to talk about things but being sleepy it did not make any sense.

My brother used to sleepwalk downstairs and one time he came downstairs as I was watching television one evening with my parents. He walked past me with his eyes open, went straight to the kitchen, made a bowl of cereal and came back and sat next to me on the settee. He ate his cereal whilst his eyes were open staring ahead of him, not even to look down at his food. My mum told me he does this a lot and I was not to disturb him. Once he had eaten his cereal, I then took him by the arm and took him to bed without talking to him.

My sister was a very nervous child and she too wet the bed, due to her being born with a smaller bladder. The atmosphere was so tense you were scared to sleep. This was due to hearing the stairs creaking and thinking 'Is my dad going to come in and belt us because we did not do a chore' or, as I said before, the milk bottles were not put out etc. It could also be that he was going upstairs to go to the toilet etc.
We used to hear my mum tell my dad that one of us had not done something, so of course you had an idea at some point that you were going to get punished for it. I

used to listen out for my dad walking up the stairs and wonder if he would be coming in to see us. I used to hear my sister crying under her covers, thinking dad was coming into our bedroom. I used to say to her 'Don't cry, and once it's done, we can then sleep'. My sister would cry during the punishment and when it was my turn, I would grit my teeth and say to myself, I will not cry. Sometimes we were belted when we were asleep so with the first whip you felt it and with that you woke up sharply.

Due to these events, it aggravated my sister's mental and emotional wellbeing. She had to lie on two aluminium mesh sheets under her bed sheet and these were attached to an alarm that went off as soon as liquid came into contact with the mesh. The alarm was meant to wake her up. She slept hard sometimes as she stayed awake so much, through fear, but she always fell asleep eventually. I would wake her up when the alarm went off and take her to the toilet. We would wash her bed sheets in the bath and tried to be quiet so as not to wake our parents. She would cry in fear and I used to tell her to keep quiet as they will hear her. The wrung-out bed sheet would then be in our room hidden under her bed to dry.

In my own way I struggled, I was protecting my sister

and my brother from my parents. There were a few times I was kicked across the room from the kitchen door and across the full length of the living room to the door, because I did not do something or just for the fun of it. On occasions, my mum would sit on a chair in the living room and carried on knitting etc and not say anything to stop it. My brother had the same treatment once. I remember when I was about nine years old, my mum said to me 'If Maria was a boy then you would not have been born as we did not want girls'. Cannot say much to that in reply to her.

My brother was bullied in the street by his so-called friends. They knew he was mentally and physically slower than them and they used to do horrible things to him. He would come home in tears and I would run out of the door and find them laughing. I would tell them to leave him alone as they knew he was young for his age. They knew I would come out to see them as they used to wait for me around the corner. I was four years older than them, but all I could do was warn them off verbally.

One day my brother came home from junior school and asked my mum 'What is a cretin?', his teacher had called him this word. I was in the room when my brother told her. I asked my mother what it meant as I was about twelve years old then. She told me what it meant and because he was still slow for his age, it was especially hurtful. I had the same teacher at Junior School, and she was a bully then. She would throw wooden blackboard erasers at our heads, call the pupils nasty names and then make you stand on your chair to make you look like an idiot if you had got maths sums wrong.

The following day, instead of walking to my senior school, I went to see my old teacher at the junior school. I went to the staff room and asked for her, but the teacher's there would not acknowledge whether she was there or not. This got the better of me and I stormed into the room and found her in the staff room. I confronted the teacher in question and firmly told her that she does not call my brother a cretin, especially as he was born mentally slow (due to being born prematurely and from lack of oxygen). I told her that she had upset both my mother and I. Her peers looked on at her and she did not say a thing to me. I walked back out of the room and never went back to that school again. She did not call my brother any names after that. I was late for my school, so I sneaked into a later class.

3. *This Is Life*

I must say that during those times at home when it was unpredictable and tough, we siblings made our own fun. We used to make games out of cereal boxes. I remember making an elaborate game with about three boxes and probably three rolls of sellotape, with marbles to go with it. It was the poor man's version of a game that was around in the early 1970s. We were very creative as money was tight.

We would play outside until there was no choice but to go back home. Bringing frog spawn back in a jar for my mum, which was not the brightest of ideas. I would take home a sprig of blossom. Mum would throw it outside and said it was bad luck to bring it into the house. I gave up bringing "presents" home after that. I used to make candles and I believe my mum has still kept one of them to this day. My sister and I also made rose water out of tap water and rose petals, thinking it would turn into perfume overnight.

My sister, brother and I used to go for a walk to the Lickey Hills, especially in the summer. It is a large country park with one hundred steps which were steps cut into a hill and I used to run up them like a mountain goat only to lie down on the grass at the top, to get my breath back. It was quite a trek to walk but we were young. We used to take the portable radio and sang when a good record came on.

My sister became a book worm and stayed in all day to read a book in between chores, if we did not do our chores then god help you, and on Sunday's we had to do the housework before our parents came down at 9am. After that, your time was your time and I would be out all day with my brother. We had a very close relationship. We were very good friends. My sister and I were like Tom and Jerry. We got into some scrapes doing daft things.

When I was in my first year at senior school, I really did not enjoy it. I would go off and do my own thing at dinnertime. Some older girls were meeting boys from the boy's school up the road. I would go with my friend Carol to her house to eat my jam sandwiches that I had made for dinner.

One of my outside adventures happened when I thought I was some kind of athlete and decided with a group of girls to pole vault over the stream at the back of our school with a very large branch. Everyone in front of me was swinging across with ease and they put the pole in the right area of the stream. When it came to me, I noticed that the girl before me had forgotten to put the pole back in the usual place. As soon as I took off, literally, I was halfway over the stream, and realising that I was not going to make the full journey. Next thing I knew was that I was heading face first into the stream and the rest is history. I got up and there was not an inch of me that was dry. I slushed back into school and tried to dry myself off with paper towels but to no avail. I noticed that there was a towel at the hand washing sinks so I used that to dry my legs and arms and sure enough as my luck would have it, a prefect of the sternest kind saw me drying my legs with the towel.

Since there was a rule not to dry your shoes with the towels, she automatically assumed I was doing that being a first-year pupil. I was then summoned to the headmistress's room faster than I could walk. The cane was out ready for me and so was the offending item, the towel. She told me off and I tried to explain to her that the prefect thought she saw me drying my shoes instead of my legs and I didn't break any rules. She was not listening, she said I was to take the towel home and show my mother what I had done and then to bring it back washed the next day. I thought 'I'm in trouble now'. I took it home, washed it and took it upstairs to my bedroom to dry as I did not want my mother to see it, because if she did and told my father then all hell would break loose. I did try to live as a child when I could.

I had known Carol since junior school, we would always sit next to each other. I would go to her house after my tea and first thing in the morning we would walk to school together. In the senior school we were in different classes. Her mother was a good woman but a no-nonsense woman and being shy in my early years I would be a little unnerved, as she said it how it was, unlike my upbringing where you did not know where you were.

She let me stay at her house in the daytime and chat to Carol and we would go out and about. On a Sunday, Carol's family all met up in a pub called The Crown, in a place called Alvechurch which is a lovely village only a few miles away from where we lived. Carol and I used to walk everywhere, and this walk was a treat especially in the summer. Firstly, we used to go to her Grandparents' house which was old and had a real log fire, which I used to stare into and try to make pictures out of the dancing flames. They were a lovely and friendly couple. Her Nan was straight talking but kind and her granddad had lovely kind eyes. Once the visit was over, we then moved on to another pub in the same village. I met her uncle Nick and aunt Margaret, and Carol's mum and dad would congregate around the bar or outside laughing loudly and enjoying themselves. Carol, myself and her brothers used to play on the rolling hills, we would roll down the hill and be covered in grass and be children with not a care in the world. We would have pop and crisps and I would forget about my life at home.

Sometimes you have to look for and savour the breaks you get in life. Make your happiness when and where you can. These memories are something I will always cherish, and I am not sure if her parents ever knew how much it meant to me to be involved in her family.

Once I got into my teenage years, I started to speak up more with people I knew. I went to Carol's house at teatime, as her mum worked at the local hospital in the evenings. I used to help Carol to feed, bathe and entertain her two younger brothers. We used to play Velcro darts and play games, as well as the usual tantrums and excuses to delay bedtime. Carol used to take them to bed. Once Carol's dad came home from working late, I would then go home which was at the time that I was due to be home by and no later.

We had lots of laughs and got into all sorts of harmless bother. I was the joker and Carol went along with it. The one time whilst her parents were out, I decided in my 'Not thought it through' mind, I would go from the top of her stairs on my hands and my legs would follow behind me. Well, I started going down the stairs on my hands slowly but as I turned on the bend of the landing, it was then that I realised that the stairs were on a straight run. I started to quicken my pace and then gravity took hold and I was going down the stairs head first, like a bullet out of a gun. It was like a bob ski or a slalom and I was catapulted headfirst down the stairs. As I got to the lower stairs, I then saw I was heading for the glass front door which did not appeal to me, so I quickly flicked my head to the side and missed the door only to hit the big, hard wooden cupboard next to the glass door and thought this was going to hurt. I hit my head and my body followed in a heap. Carol ran down the stairs and shouted to me to see if I was still alive and all I could do was laugh and tears rolled down my face, whilst I was seeing stars around me like in the cartoons. I was a little clumsy during my visits there.

One time I was in Carol's garden and I was about to sit down on her mum's gold coloured deckchair, where the material hangs low to the ground like you used to see at the seaside years ago. I must have sat down a little too low and all of a sudden, I heard this loud rip and then I was sitting on the ground with the material of the deckchair around me. I started to laugh with embarrassment and her mum's face was a picture. She shouted at me for wrecking her deckchair, but I could not hold the laughter in, be it nerves as she was a formidable woman, but she had a good heart. I think after a few seconds, we all laughed thank goodness, as I could not afford to pay for another deckchair for her on my newspaper round money. I was only seven stone in weight, wet through or eight stone with rocks in my pockets, so god only knows how I did it, there was no meat on me.

The one time I had to think on my feet fast at her house or suffer the consequences was when I was trying to be on my best behaviour, as her mum used to say I was a bad influence on Carol. One-day Carol and I were out and about, and we walked to her house. She then realised that she had locked herself out and the keys were in the house somewhere. 'What a bright thing to do' I said jokingly. She was concerned though as her mum was due back some time soonish. We walked around to the back of the house, but no windows were open and then we went around to the side of the house and I saw that a very small window in the kitchen was open. I thought that this was the only way we could get in. Carol was only five feet tall and I was about five feet six, so we knew then who was going to attempt it. I asked her to give me a 'bunk up', a term to mean to crouch down a little and too cup her hands together, with this I could stand on her hands and she could help me up the wall with a push.

I would not make a burglar as it was like a comedy of errors. We were like Laurel and Hardy as friends. I fell out of her hands and landed face first into the wall, not a pretty look. Carol started to panic as her mum was coming home soon and we had to do this! After a bit of examination of our technique we tried again, to launch me up and push me against the wall, so I could grab the outside window ledge. I went up and grabbed the ledge and held on tightly but then put my hand over the inside of the window and pulled myself up. I did think at this point I could get a job in the circus. I then stuck my head into the open window and tried to reach for the taps of the sink so I could pull myself further into the kitchen. That's when my plan went wrong. The window was small and narrow with a catch arm, which you place on top of a metal point on the window frame, allowing you to keep it open in the right place.

I pulled myself forward to get in, I realised that I could not move at all and was in a lot of pain down the intimate part of my body. I had my best Brutus flared jeans on. When I was wearing them, I felt that I was the best thing since sliced bread and looked really fashionable, this was the 1970s! The metal peg that stuck up on the frame was stuck in the fly of my jeans and was going nowhere other than giving me pain in a place it should not have been, causing my eyes to water. Carol did not know this and was wondering why I was bobbing up and down with my head in the kitchen and my bottom and legs outside in the air. Not a pretty sight. I yelled 'I'm stuck on the bloody metal peg and it's hurting me' at the same time laughing nervously. Why do we laugh when we are nervous or in trouble? Carol then said, "I will go and get some help". I thought 'Thank god and hurry as I am in a lot of pain now'. I was not going to shift. I must have looked like one of those seaside jokes at that time, with a bird on the side of a drinking glass bobbing in and out of the glass.

Not long after this I heard Carol come back with someone but could not hear their voice, so I was none the wiser whom she had brought back. All of a sudden, I felt a big pair of hands around my bottom cheeks and I thought in that second, 'Who is that?'. I was then shoved from behind, from my bottom cheeks with such force. I shot through the window, headfirst in the sink. Potted plants that were on the windowsill, had then been strewn across the floor and somehow, whilst my head was in the sink, I flipped my body over and I landed on the floor with the potted plants, a little dazed. It was a proper gymnastic flip too! I had not done gymnastics before, but I was definitely flexible! I got up quickly and I ran to the front door and let Carol in so we could tidy up the mess in the kitchen. It was then I saw who was with Carol, whose big hands had held my bottom cheeks and pushed me with such gusto. It was her next-door neighbour who surprisingly was a woman. I thanked her as I was a bit embarrassed about her holding my bottom etc. She left and once alone, Carol said, 'She lives with a woman too', in the 1970s it was not known or so open as it is now to be in a same sex relationship. She laughed her head off as I said to her 'Could you not have found a man?', but then thinking on, a man holding my teenage bottom is not good either! It was a comedy situation for sure. I did have good times with my friend and we still have maintained our friendship throughout our lives.

4. *Teenage Angst*

As I got to my teenage years, I would experience more premonitions and spirit visitations. It was the 21st of November 1974 and I was eleven years old. The events of this night nearly changed my childhood and my life. It was my dad's birthday and he went to work as per usual. He worked in Birmingham City Centre and had worked overtime for a couple of hours, he normally got home at 6pm. It was evening time and all the family were home, apart from my dad. He had left work at about 7.30 pm. He rang my mum, as we had a telephone in the house in those days, and said he was going to go for a drink in the Tavern In The Town pub for a bit and then he would set off home.

He walked to the Tavern In The Town pub with the intention of having a few pints and to celebrate his birthday. He got there for about 8.10pm. He put his hand on the door handle of the pub and pulled it open and went into the top part of the pub. All of a sudden, he heard a voice in his head, saying "Go home to your family". My dad told me years later that he did not know who the voice was, nor how it happened as he did not believe in spirit or guides intervention. He stopped in his tracks, halfway into the pub. You entered it at street level, but you had to walk down a set of stairs to the basement of the bar. It was all closed off from the street. Once he heard this voice, he felt it persuaded him enough to think about it. He turned around and went out of the pub door and walked towards his bus stop to get a bus home. He would have walked past another pub called the Mulberry Bush, on the way to his bus. At 8.17pm walking past the Mulberry Bush pub, a bomb went off and at 8.27pm, the Tavern In The Town pub was no more.

Allegedly, some members of the IRA who had a group in Birmingham, and later confirmed in the newspaper, had planted bags with bombs in them earlier in the evening, in the Mulberry Bush and Tavern In The Town. The people in the Tavern In The Town would not have heard or felt the bomb go off in the Mulberry Bush as that bomb went off at about 8.17pm and with them being under street level, they did not know to flee the city centre. My mum, my sister and I were watching television and all of a sudden, our programme was interrupted, when a news flash came up on the screen. The man on the television was to say that bombs had gone off in two Birmingham City Centre pubs and then proceeded to say which ones they were. My mum said that our dad was in the Tavern In The Town, one of the pubs. It was a complete shock. We all sat there dumbstruck. We did not speak but just waited for more information from the newsreader on the television or our local radio station BRMB. I could not take in the reality of the situation, let alone what had happened to my dad.

At about 9pm my dad walked through the front door and we all looked at each other. My mum got upset and told him what had happened and then the news came on telling us all the details. My dad did not have a clue about what had happened. He had missed the bombings by seven and seventeen minutes. He said he walked past the Mulberry Bush pub and a few minutes later he was near New Street Station when he felt the earth shake and thought it was the trains, that was the first bomb going off. He did not say a lot after the news announcements and the film footage of the aftermath on that night. We were sent to bed and did not talk about it.

It made me think that bad things happen, and it came too close to home for me. I would not have had a dad. What would have happened to us as a family? Even as an eleven-year old, I felt for the people and the families who were affected by it. I went to school the next day and that was all that was talked about. Some said that they knew somebody who was affected. I did not say what nearly happened to my family. I knew that my dad was in one of the pubs but only when I was older, he admits to me about the voice persuading him to leave the pub. He was a strong man and a character and did not believe in things like the paranormal, but this person must have been stronger than him in this instance. My dad did not talk about it and yet I did not see this happening either.

During my time at an all-girls senior school, I was seen to be different. I was quieter than the other girls and didn't want to be there and I went into myself. To get away from things I would go to school, get my name called for the register and then as we walked to the next class, I would run through the gates and make my escape. I would walk around the shopping centre near the school, walk to a stream in a poor housing estate, where I saw my first and only sewer rat. I thought it was a cat as it was all wet and sleek and it was very big. Sometimes I would go back home as my parents were at work.

This worked well, until one day I made my way home on the bus one morning and as I was getting off the bus, I realised my mum was in the queue to get on the bus. I thought 'What the hell am I going to say to her when she sees me?'. So, my mind was rambling, thinking I have left my geography book at home etc. mum was staring straight at me. My heart was racing thinking "I'm in trouble now" and as I went to go past her, she continued to stare ahead and then got on the bus. I thought 'Am I invisible? Can she not see me?'. I remember as children we used to pretend that we were invisible if we were fearful or in trouble. I walked on towards home thinking about what had just happened and continued to be puzzled by it all but also relieved.

Things were bad at school and I had been playing truant for some months. The education officer visited my mother and told her that I had not attended school. This did not go down well, as well as the obvious punishment for this, I was also sent down a class which was to be the worst thing they could have done. The class they put me in was with bullies who gave out actual physical violence. If you were quiet, they saw that as a weakness, something to toy with. I would be grabbed by a few girls and being so light in weight, due to the jam sandwiches for tea and was playfully called 'Tin Ribs'. I would be thrown into the air and dropped mid-air to land hard on the ground, other girls had this treatment too. A bit like Flashman out of the Tom Brown's Schooldays novel. Teachers were frightened of the group of girls and did not do anything, knowing that we were being bullied most days. Some of the bullies were being mistreated at home I believe, so they took it out on the others in the class. I too was having a time of it at home but did not resort to this.

Outside the school no one knew this was going on, my parents would not have gone to the school, so it was put up and shut up. It got too much for me as I was getting bullied at home and at school and could not escape it. I was strong on the outside but struggled on the inside. So, at the age of fourteen, after a punishment too many, I took the only way out of this world that I could see. I was away from home, so I took a load of tablets which took their time to affect me. I can actually say that way is slow, and you have more time to think about your actions. I heard the noises that I get when I leave my body when I am about to sleep, and I also felt everything in my body slowing down. Once I felt I was under the influence of them, I then walked out of the room I was in and went outside to get away. A friend of mine saw me and she realised I was in trouble as I passed out in front of her.

An ambulance was called, and I do remember being in it, but after that I do not know anything that happened afterwards, but what I do know is that I left my body and was up and away. Then I was travelling very fast through a colourful tunnel, within its twists and turns. It felt like I was not going to get to the end of it. It was quiet and I didn't have time to think about where I was. I then stopped abruptly, and I was standing alone in a dark area. No one else was there, just me. That is when I realised, I was not in a familiar place and I started to get a little scared. I then looked in front of me and saw what appeared to be two heavy looking doors and they started to open. As this was happening, a white light so bright, that I could not look at it appeared. It was coming through the space in between the doors as it was opening. Once the doors had opened, I was pushed forwards towards the light by a strong force. I then saw someone in silhouette form standing in the beam of the light so I could not see who it was. They were waiting for me.

It followed that I was sitting down on a chair which had the appearance of a throne next to a man with long white hair, a long straggly beard and whilst wearing a long white robe. He did not talk to me with his mouth, but he spoke to me with his mind. I could hear his voice in my head and his thoughts. We communicated that way for a while and then in front of me, was a projection like film. He showed me some episodes from my fourteen years of life. He showed me the incident when my brother was a toddler, he had an accident and nearly died. It was due to me not looking where I had put my bike. I saw things that were good, and I saw some things which were not. This was to show the balance of my life and my deeds. It is called a Life Review. Throughout my time with him, with no one else around in the quiet surroundings, I felt I was in the presence of someone in authority.

Once this was over, I remember being back in the dark area again all alone. All of a sudden, a lady spoke in my ear very softly and told me 'It is not your time and you have to go back' and said this three times. As soon as she said this, I was pulled back by such force, that I did not have time to think about what she said. It was like being pulled backwards by a bungee rope. As I was going backwards, I once again fell down the colourful tunnel, passing all the colours of the rainbow, and then with a bang, I landed on something hard. It was the hospital trolley in A&E. I had returned back to where I did not want to be and in a hospital too. I gradually opened my eyes to see a doctor looking over me and with my parents standing at the end of my feet, he said to them, 'She is back'.

Once I came around, the doctor had told me that when I

first came back to life, he asked me if I knew who the people at the end of my feet were and I said 'No'. I did not know them. I did not recognise my parents which he thought was strange. Once I came around properly to the land of the living, I recognised them. The doctor did not mention that I had died and returned, and it was not spoken about ever again in my family. I was aggrieved that I came back as I wanted to stay in another place. So, after that event, I was to change dramatically.

LIVING IN TWO WORLDS

5. *Back To Earth*

It was 1977, I was fourteen and I was rebelling against people who did not understand me including my parents. This was the punk era that came at the right time for me. I went to a school friend's house one evening and was later home than I should have been. I thought it best to ring home and tell them I would get home later. I waited outside a phone box as someone was using the phone. Then all of a sudden, I looked up into the dark skies and saw something hovering over a house for what seemed like a couple of minutes or so. It was dome shaped, but the lights were on the side of it in a strip and it was rotating at a speed that made the colours seem a bit of a blur. Not red and blue like planes but different colours. It made no sound and was very visible in the dusk of the evening and the size of it was large but not to the size of a plane or helicopter. After staring at it for a long time thinking what that is and why is it hovering way above the roof of the house, I soon realised that this was not normal. It then sped off with such speed and at an angle that you could not follow it with your eyes because it was so fast. Throughout this sighting, there was no sound and I thought I was the only one who saw it. I rang my parents up and told them what I saw, and it was the usual "get yourself home now" and not believing me thinking it was a teenager's imagination. I got home and the local radio station was on and it seems that people were calling up the station and saying they saw something like I did too. I thought thank god for that I wasn't going mad. No one could explain it and said that they thought it was a U.F.O.

As a fourteen-year-old girl, I was at the stage of seeing boyfriends, and my family started to notice that I was being different. I would go off into my own world and write poetry, go out for walks in the countryside where before I would play in the street or see my friends etc. I seemed to be stronger almost to the point of resilience towards my class bullies. They did not know what to do with me. My parents did not know what to do with me. It was almost like part of me was still at the other place I left behind, and the other part of me was doing its time on this earth. I started to have premonitions of things that were going to happen to my family or have weird dreams. I did not fear my father anymore, it was almost like he could not break my spirit. He still continued to rule the house with his way, but I stayed out of the house a lot more and it got to the point that the mental mind games were no longer affecting me any more like it did my siblings. If I did not ask his permission before 8pm for me to go out the next day to see my friends, then I did not go out. I used to learn my lines like an actor or actress before they walked out on to the stage. Before the NDE (Near Death Experience), I would have had to rehearse what I would have to say and if I bottled it then I did not ask. My dad was still taking out his anger on the children and still continued to belt us. He stopped kicking me across the living room from one end to the other, but he belted me less so.

One day my brother forgot to do one of his chores and he ran across the living room to where I was sitting and tried to get through the door to get out. The door would not open in time and then I saw my father coming for him. I ran and stood in front of my brother, who by then was shaking in fear, with my arms stretched out. My father stood in front of me and started to take his belt off, he was wrapping it around his fist. He told me to 'Get out of the way!' and I said 'No'. I then said to my father 'you will have to get through me first before you get to him'.
He was shocked at my outburst. It was the first time I had stood up to him. He looked at me in such anger, with his fist near me, stood for a few seconds looking at me and

then said, 'you're not worth it' and turned around and walked out of the back door. My brother fell back into the door with fear and relief. He was shocked at what I had said but not as much as I was, but this was the turning point for me. My father did not speak to me for a few days or acknowledge me due to my outburst. I think he realised that I would stand up for myself and he saw an anger in me that was like him.

Life went on and I stayed at my nan's a lot more, when I could. The visits from spirits at my nan's house got stronger but I noticed that the negative energy was stronger too. This was when I noticed that my uncle who lived with my grandparents was acting strangely. He was a hippy in the 1960s and took certain drugs and then he went through a phase of being a 'Hells Angel'. He had tattoos on his body and mixed with the wrong crowd. We were not sure if it was the drugs he took, or if he had dabbled with the occult. My nan realised that he was schizophrenic, and he had episodes of being violent to her. I got on with my uncle, but I too saw that side of him.

I went to knock on his bedroom once and when he opened the door, his face was different. His face was dark, and he shouted at me to get away from his door. The dark energy was on the landing near his bedroom. He would not take his medication for schizophrenia, so his behaviour was erratic. He had to have metal bars installed on his bedroom window to stop him jumping out of the window into the yard. You could have cut the air with a knife, but I loved my grandparents and I wanted to stay with them regardless of the negativity in the house. So, this was my first experience of seeing and feeling negative energy and its effects on people. I went back home, and my psychic gifts came back with me.

One day something tragic happened to one of the families in our street, one of their sons had died in a freak accident by drowning in a river. I knew him but he was a lot older than me. A few weeks later as I was in my bedroom, I was about to turn the bedroom light out as my sister was in bed. I saw in the corner of the room, a young lad, very tall, and was wearing a shirt and jeans and looking at me. My sister did not see him, so I said, 'Look it's Alan' she thought I was mad, and I was scaring her, yet I could not convince her that he was definitely in the room. He opened his mouth to say something, but I couldn't hear what he was saying. He then disappeared and my sister went to sleep. I told my mum the next day and was told in no uncertain terms never to mention it again as it did not happen!

I continued to see spirits in the house and by acknowledging them was my way of communicating to them. I used to know what my mother was going to say and how she felt. It was strange that I was picking up on her. I saw things for other people but not myself. My mother went through a phase herself of wanting to know about the paranormal as she had the gift too, but she did not want to acknowledge it. Unfortunately, she started to read books that led her down the wrong path of paranormal and she delved into the occult instead. This went on for a few years, when I was a child and into my teenage years and it was an unnerving time for us in the home. I am not sure if my siblings knew what was going on with her, but I did. She had the look of my uncle, a look that went through you and you knew it was not them totally. She had long black hair, black eye pencil around her eyes and very long sharp fingernails. When I was a young child, she would grab my hands and dig her long nails into my palms and say, 'I am going to hurt you and make you cry.' She would not let go until I wriggled away from her grasp.

She would tell my sister that she would not be at home when she got back from infants and junior school as she will be gone, which totally upset my sister. With me though she knew I was different. I used to read the books she left on the bookshelf and one day in the bath after reading one about witchcraft, I found myself looking for the signs of the devil on me. That is when I realised these books are dangerous and did not pick them up again. The other books were written by Dennis Wheatley and also reference books on the occult. My mum was absolutely involved in this way of life. I tried to talk to her and tell her that this is bad, but she was too far into it. Then one day I came home and noticed that the books had gone, she had locked them away in a cupboard. I asked her what had happened, and she told me that she was seeing horrible faces at the windows and other sinister events were happening to her and she was scared.

After that, every Tuesday afternoon I would come home from school to find my mum entertaining two ladies from the church in our living room who were reading sections from the bible. They read to mum and she listened. She threw herself into these visits and I realised that she wanted no part of her search for the paranormal anymore as she saw things not of this earth, she later confessed to me. My sister and I were made to go to church every Sunday after her close call with negative work. She probably thought I would go the same way, but I did not work that way. She was aware of how I was and would confide in me with certain things.

When my brother was about ten years old, he started being rebellious to get attention etc. She wanted to send my brother away to the Children's Home for Wayward Children that was run by nuns. She had contacted them with a request to have my brother and she showed me the letter of acceptance from the Children's Home. I told her that she can't send him away, it's her son, but she was adamant. I then said, 'Look I will straighten him out but don't send him there'. She relented and it was not spoken about ever again. I believe my sister does not know to this day.

My brother and I were close so I was hoping it would work. I still protected my brother. At this stage I was seeing boyfriends and I was going to the cinema, thinking I would marry one day etc but that would come and go as I went from one boyfriend to another not knowing what it was about. I did attract wayward boys not afraid to be themselves and as it was the punk era, it fuelled my rebellious streak. One time I was late coming home from a date, and we missed the last bus home from the city centre of Birmingham, so it was a ten mile walk home. I rang my parents to tell them we were having to walk home but it didn't cut ice. So, when we eventually made it to my front path, I gave my boyfriend a head-start to run down the road before my father got to him. It worked as he was down the street when I opened the door with my key and sure enough, he was there to clatter me one as he couldn't lay his hands on my boyfriend.

I left school at sixteen and it wasn't soon enough for me and started work straight away. I was working as an office junior in a large firm. In work I was a different person, I was quiet and knew how to behave in the world of work, not like school. During this time life at home was still fraught with mental, emotional and physical punishments dished out. During this time, I met a lad who was three years older than me and worked in the same workplace. He was a strong character and he would tell me he would look after me. Being sixteen you do not know any better, and he met my parents and knew what was going on at home. He said to me a few times 'Come live with me and I will look after you'. It was like a lifeline from escaping the confines of home. Someone promising you a better life.

Then one night at home I was in the kitchen with my mum and I was washing up when I heard the door open behind me. It was my Dad and he was angry about me not doing something, he was going on and on at me and I had had enough so I said under my breath 'get off my back'. He didn't hear what I had said as he said 'what did you say' so he asked my mum what I had said, she was about to tell him when I said again in a louder and braver voice 'get off my back'. I heard him taking his belt off to hit me and since my hands were in the washing up bowl, I grabbed the first thing that was under the sudsy water, it was a knife. I turned around on my heels quickly with no fear, and when I saw the belt wrapped around his fist, I said 'don't you dare come near me' with the knife pointing at him. I was so far gone, adrenalin pumping, I knew I had to protect myself. He looked at me and saw in my eyes that I was not joking. He walked away and as soon as he did, I turned around and carried on washing up.

The next day I knew I had to leave home, so I saw my boyfriend and said I would live with him as I had nowhere else to go and he promised to look after me and would not treat me like my dad. As I was leaving home, my dad said to me 'you made your bed now you lie in it' which basically means you made your decision and there is no going back on it. After I left home I did not see or speak to my parents as they had disowned me.

LIVING IN TWO WORLDS

6. *Hell On Earth*

For the first couple of weeks with 'Dave', we were like a normal couple and lived in his council flat. We saw each other at the workplace and at home. I noticed he was getting possessive with me, he was watchful of who I spoke to at work and accused me of silly things, saying I was too friendly with my male colleagues etc. I was isolated from my family and friends as I was his property and he told people of that fact. I wasn't allowed out socially and everywhere I went, so did he as his paranoia and possessiveness took over. If he felt a man was looking at me then he would say something to the man, to ward them off, grab my arm and drag me home and then I got accused of bringing the attention to myself and he then made sure my face was not one that any man would look at. He would hit and punch me in the face so I could not go out like that.

At home he became controlling and violent. If the bacon was not cooked right or if I looked at him in a way that he felt was wrong, then he would punch and kick me to the floor. I had to think ahead like I was at home again. I had to think of what could set him off and to avoid it.

I had to come off the contraceptive pill as he wanted us to have a baby so I would not leave him. I took the tablets and hid them, but he found them, and he flushed them down the toilet and threatened me if I ever did this again then I would not live long. The one day I had a gold ingot which was mine and he demanded it for himself. I tried to explain to him that he could have it but there was no chain. Because I answered him back, he then blew up and punched me to the floor and then started kicking me in the stomach and then whilst I was lying on the floor, he started treading on me with his boots on. He stopped momentarily so I started to try and sit up to get up to get away from him, so he then kicked my left shoulder so far back that it was dislocated. He walked out of the flat and slammed the door. I had to sit up again and bring my shoulder forward to click it into place again.

The assaults were a regular occurrence and so were the sexual attacks too, either after a good hiding where I had to make out I loved him and I was enjoying what he did or grit my teeth and endure it as there was no consent, it was rape yet in society at the time, rape in relationships or marriage did not exist, apparently! One night he ripped up my normal clothes, not my office work clothes, with his bare hands, I wore these to go out with him to the pub etc and broke the heels off my shoes and he said, 'you cannot leave me now'.

One afternoon I had to run an errand for my boss to go

and get some stationary from the suppliers in the city centre and Dave saw me and said I was meeting someone. In his work he had to use a dumper truck and as soon as I said I was not seeing someone I was running an errand, he swung round and got the metal bar from the dumper truck which is a turn handle for the dumper truck and hit me across the face with it. I heard a crunch against my cheekbone and knew that would leave a mark. I ran out of his way and went to the shop to get the stationary. When I got back to work my workmates asked me where I got my mark from on my face. As usual you say you had an accident, but they knew what was going on, with all my black eyes and bruises on my face over the months.

When Dave got home, he was angry and blamed me for him losing his job as his boss saw the incident and sacked him on the spot. It was my fault apparently. It was Hell to play that night.

I endured every day with this kind of behaviour but still went to work, bringing my wage home for him to spend it on drink. He used to lash out when he was sober then

go out drinking only for him to come home and start attacking me again. There was nowhere for me to go as I knew he would look for me.

One day I went out and bumped into my sister who I had not seen for months, she asked me how I was doing. She told me that she could not cope with me not being at home as it was still bad there. So, she left home to live in a bedsit and was seeing a really nice guy who had his own bedsit too. Years later she admitted that I looked shocking and scared. I did not tell her what was going on.

Then one morning after he beat me and savaged me, I lay in bed awake as he was asleep next to me. I could take no more as I knew he would end up killing me and at that point I thought it would be a release. All of a sudden, I saw standing next to my side of the bed three very tall figures, all in white gowns, bright golden light emanating from them. They were talking to themselves but not through their mouths but like telepathy, but I could hear them. They said, 'she cannot take any more and she must get out'. I heard it loud and clear, I was not imagining this. I was in awe of these beings yet frightened in case he woke up and saw me looking at them. I could not explain this to him. I looked at them and then they disappeared. I knew I had to find the courage to leave but did not know when or how before it was too late.

Things escalated and he was making a nuisance of himself at my work. He threatened people who dared talk to me, so by doing this they knew what he was doing to me. One dinnertime I was in the pub that was on the work premises with my work colleagues and I saw him outside through the window. He beckoned me to come outside and started arguing with me, demanding what I was doing in there. I explained I was having my dinner with my boss and work colleagues, when he started punching me and throwing me against the brick wall. A Dutch lorry driver who was parked up near the pub who was delivering his goods to our firm, saw him do this and shouted at him to stop. Dave then shouted to him that I was his property and he could do what he wanted with me.

As he was attacking me, I was trying to grab the handle of the pub door to try and get away from him and maybe to get someone's attention in the pub, but I was fingertips away from it. The man ran off and so did Dave. I did not know the Dutch man had run off to get the security men. I got myself to the door and stumbled in and fell to the floor. All of a sudden, I heard a furore in the pub, it was the market lads. They did not need to know what had happened but off they ran out of the door. They went out looking for him. I was taken to the toilet by my workmates and they cleaned my face up. It was bloody and I had a start of a black eye. I was in shock and embarrassed that people had seen me like that as it normally happened at home and I thought I had hidden it well, so I thought. One friend said to me 'you cannot go back home to this as he will kill you'. I said that I agreed but where would I go? I got cleaned up and I was taken back to the office where I was spoken to and tried to get my head around what had happened and where to go for safety. A male colleague offered me his couch for the night and said his wife would not mind but I decided to decline as I did not want to put them out.

My boss said to go and see my parents who I had not seen since I left home many months previously. I found out that he had rung my mum and said to her to take me in as I was in a bad way. This was a step that I did not want to do but I felt I had no choice.

I went to see my mum and she said, 'you can't stay here', then my dad came home and saw me. He said, 'What is she doing here, get her out of my house!'. I tried to explain to my dad I had nowhere to go and he said it was my problem. I left the house and got a bus to the city centre. I was just walking around not knowing what to do.

It was getting dark and cold. All I had was the clothes on my back and no coat. I decided to bed down for the night in a shop doorway, better than being on a bench and hopefully keep out of sight from people and I would be dry as it started to rain. I was just sitting there thinking this is it and I have got to keep my wits about me as I am on my own. I am seventeen and people will see me as a child.All of a sudden, my nan came into my head and I had this overwhelming feeling to ring her, it was about 9pm and I thought I would wake her up if I rang her. Then I thought I would tell her where I am in case anything happened to me. I rang her and she knew something was wrong. She told me to get to her house as soon as possible, and in no uncertain terms so I could stay with her until I got back on my feet.

I got the bus with what money I had in my purse. I walked to my nan's house and for the first time I felt safe. My nan stayed up with me most of the night talking about what had been happening as I think my grandad thought it was best for my nan to talk to me alone about personal things. My nan had a walking stick as she had arthritis in her knees, but she was still feisty. I explained that I did not want to get my grandparents involved as he was violent, she grabbed her stick and waved it in the air and said if he comes to her house then she will give him 'what for' with it. I could well believe she would do that too.

The next day after a very restless night, my nan and I went to the shops near her home which is the opposite side of the city where I had lived and many miles apart from the area of where the flat was. We were walking around the clothes shops as I had no clothes other than the ones I wore the day before which I was still wearing.

We got to the till and all of a sudden, I heard a voice I recognised behind me. It was a neighbour from the flat I lived in and she recognised me and said that Dave was looking for me and my heart and stomach was filled with dread. I could not believe that I was miles away from the flat and yet this neighbour was shopping in this area.

My nan said to the neighbour to tell him to leave me alone, but I knew in my heart this was not the end of it. She would get back to him and tell him which area I was in. I knew then I had to get away from the area and lay low somewhere else. We got back to my nan's house and I told her I loved her and I did not want to bring any trouble to her door and she reiterated that if he came to the house, then she would give him what for with her stick and I hugged her and said nan he is dangerous he would not stop at attacking you too. She relented and said to look after myself and let me know where I was and how I was doing. I got changed and put on my new clothes and put the remaining new clothes she bought me in a carrier bag and got a bus to the city centre. I walked aimlessly around the city centre until I went to my sister's place of work. I told her what had happened, and she said I could stay at her boyfriend's bedsit until I could get myself back on my feet. I was so grateful but worried that I would be spotted again and put somebody else in danger. She assured me that her boyfriend would be okay with it all.

LIVING IN TWO WORLDS

7. *On The Run*

I had met my sister's boyfriend Akbar before, he was ten years older than my sister and a very approachable man. He was from Persia, now called Iran and fled his country due to National Service which he did not want to do and with the overthrow of the Shah who was exiled from Persia, which caused a lot of war and problems of repression amongst his people. He came to England to study and met my sister. He had a job, and he worked all day and was self-sufficient.

She took me to his bed sit, and I was still very wary of men due to what had happened to me by the actions of men. He understood this. He explained that I could stay in the bed sit during the day and somewhere I could eat, use the bathroom and watch television but at night-time I would have to sneak into the attic in case anyone in the communal house saw me. The house was divided into six bedsits', so everyone had their own living space. I found a mattress in the attic and slept on that in the dark and god knows what else I was sleeping with up there, but it was a place of safety and no one knew I was there. I was seventeen and it was against the law for someone below the age of eighteen to live in private accommodation. The landlord was Jewish and was very hard on the tenants. This arrangement carried on for a while, talking

63

to Akbar and staying in his bedsit until bedtime and sometimes my sister would come over or he would go to her place giving me some space to think. He was a kind man and asked for no money other than to keep myself out of the way of the other tenants. I did as he asked, and it worked well for a month or two.

I had to go to court to get an injunction against Dave to order him to keep away from me. When I was in court I was called into the Judge's chambers to explain why I wanted an injunction and I said Dave was an animal and was violent so we then went back into the court and I had to stand right next to Dave whilst the injunction was read out to him. He smirked as if to say that it was not going to stop him getting to me and then in front of the judge and my solicitor, he said to me 'I will get you outside'. My solicitor heard this and told me to leave the back way out of the court.

I went back to work and tried to get on with my life, but this was to change. I came out of work one evening and started to walk the route to my bus stop to go home. Behind me all of a sudden, I heard a voice shouting 'John, get her'. I didn't have a chance to turn around to see who it was, and I was grabbed by the arms by two men and bundled into the back of a car. It happened so fast I did not have time to scream out. The car sped off and I realised it was Dave and his friend who had kidnapped me from the street. Dave was shouting at me saying 'How dare you leave me, you made me do this'. I was shocked and frightened as I did not know what he was going to do to me and where he was going to take me. They took me back to the flat we used to live in and then John left the flat. Dave assaulted me all night and then threw me in a back room where he locked me in. There was one window in the room, and I thought I could escape from there but when I looked out of the window, I realised how high up it was and if I jumped, then I would have broken my legs landing on the ground. I was kept in that room for two days, not knowing how long I will be kept in there and what he was going to do with me. He came in from time to time to give me food and drink, take me to the toilet and then proceeded to do what he wanted over again.

In those two days he beat me so badly unbeknownst to me or him that I was about two months pregnant and I miscarried in the flat. Those two days were hell on earth, knowing that no one knew where I was, and I would not be found. I was giving up on life and knew that he was not going to let me go. Then a thought from nowhere came into my head which gave me inspiration to live and the courage to plan my escape.

I shouted out to him and tried to be his friend and I said that we could start again as a couple, I still loved him, but people would be looking for me as I had not been to work, I thought I could go and get my clothes from where I was staying, not telling him where that was, and come back to the flat and be a couple again like before. He was not convinced of this action, but I had to tell him loads of times that we will be together again, but I need to go to work and get my stuff and come back. Eventually he was convinced that I would do this, and he took me to the local train station. Whilst waiting for the train he grabbed my arm and threatened to take me back to the flat as he had second thoughts. I had to think quickly as I could not go back there again as I would not come out again so I repeated that I would come back later and start again. The train did not arrive, and he was getting restless by every minute. Eventually the train came, and he still grabbed my arm not letting me get on the train, people started to look at us thinking what was going on. I said again 'I have got to go to work and I will see you later'. He let go of my arm and in my ear, he said, 'If you are lying to me, I will kill you'. I smiled and gave him a kiss goodbye and got on the train as if nothing was wrong, praying the train would leave quickly before he would change his mind and pull me off the train or get on the train to follow me.

The train began to move, and I waved to him until he was out of sight and then I started to shake with fear because of the two days I had endured and at getting out of the flat. It overwhelmed me that I was out of the flat and away from him.

I quickly got to work and told them what had happened. The police came and saw my face was bruised and took notes but said it was a domestic and could do nothing even though he had broken an injunction which would normally mean prison.

I got back to Akbar's bedsit and holed myself in for a few days until I could find the strength to go back to work and go outside. I went back to work and then one night I was in Akbar's bedsit when there was a loud knock on the front door. I couldn't open the door as I was not meant to be seen so Akbar opened the door and saw two men with baseball bats asking for me. I could hear them shouting and threatening to break his legs if he did not go and get me. He stood up to them and said that I was not coming out and called them cowards and for the way I was being mistreated. I rang the police who were situated in the next road down from there and once they heard what the drama was, they said it was a case of domestic violence, but they would still come. All I could think about was Akbar standing up to them with bats, what they would do to him and if they drag me out. They gave up as I shouted through a door 'I have called the police and they are on their way'. It took the police an hour to come when it was only a two-minute drive away.

I told them both of us could have been killed by the time they had arrived. They were not bothered.

Dave must have followed me home. I had to go and get another court injunction for him to stay away from me and Akbar's address and the judge told him it will be prison next time. I could not believe that he was going to get away with it again.

One evening I went out for a drink as I was getting my courage back, but it did waiver a bit if I heard someone walk behind me or run behind me thinking it was him. I was walking home towards the bedsit when all of a sudden, I was grabbed, and a knife was held to my throat. It was Dave who was threatening to kill me. I could not scream or do anything, he just pushed me along the road to find a quiet place. This was a prostitute area and many a time I saw men in their cars kerb crawling looking for women.

I was waiting outside a phone box to use the phone once when a man pulled up and asked me how much I charge for a certain sexual act. I told him I was waiting to use the phone, he didn't believe me.

I was pulled out of sight, a police car looking for kerb crawlers and prostitutes came up the road near me and Dave then put the knife in my coat and said 'This is yours' in case we got pulled up. This was my chance to escape so I ran as fast as I could to the bedsit and left him behind. The court injunction did not mean anything to him, he did not care.

I knew I had to move, and I did not want to put Akbar in this position anymore as he was so good to me and he saved my life which I will always be grateful for. The landlord had been tipped off that I had been living under his roof rent free and sleeping in the attic, so he threatened to either kick me out or we both would go. I explained that I had nowhere to go and I was trying to stay safe and I was not a nuisance but the landlord still wanted us out so I said 'Akbar has done nothing wrong and I will go if you can give me a day, or so'. I will always remember that landlord.

Within two days I found a place, and this was due to the landlord not knowing my age. That was my haven for a couple of years, I met a good friend called Lesley and we had some great times going and I went with her to see her family in Oxford where I realised that her family life was not like mine. It gave me stability and it got me back on my feet. I changed jobs and worked in a factory as it was more money so I could pay for luxuries like going out etc. I was at the stage though where I noticed that I had no trust in men, not surprising there! Akbar was the only one I trusted. I would talk to the lads on the shop floor, but they did not get to see the real me. I was feisty and protective of myself and would not take any hassle from a man. I took up karate lessons which were run by a six dan Japanese master who was strict but fair. I then got my confidence back to walk down the street when I was out.

I was starting to have stomach trouble and was admitted into hospital thinking it was my appendix but when they opened me up after taking my appendix out the surgeons noticed that I was damaged inside, my womb was under my bowel and I had damage to my intestines. They later told me I would not have children because of the damage that was done by Dave's treading on me and the kicking I had had to endure to my stomach. I was shattered by this as I did not want the choice to be taken away from me. They said I would need further surgery in years to come to rectify the damage.

8. *Life Goes On*

I got on with my life although I self-destructed by drinking, partying, and going out with men who I had no real trust in. I felt I was untouchable as I did not show the real me and kept my emotions under wraps. You could be with me, but you could not have me. I swore to myself that no-one was going to hurt me like I had been hurt before. I met a lovely lad who I did go out with for a while, but I told him that I was damaged goods and he needed to be with a lovely girl. He did not agree with me, but I hope he did find the one for him. I stood up to men when I should have walked off, but I had to do it.

There was one night when I saw a couple arguing in the street and the man was hitting the woman. I ran over and told him to leave her alone and she shouted to me to leave him alone as he was her partner. I couldn't believe it, I was trying to protect her, and she was protecting him. I learnt a very important lesson that night. Not all women want to be protected. I got on with my life and one day in the city centre, I saw Dave with his new family, he did not see me, but I saw the woman he was with and his two sons. He had children where he made sure I could not. After that I knew I had to turn my life around and get on with my life as best I could.

One night as I was leaving my flat, I heard a woman screaming from opposite where I was walking. She was in the street screaming 'He's got my baby; he's got my baby'. I looked up and sure enough the baby was being held out of the top window by a man who was threatening to throw the baby into the street. I shouted to her to go to the phone box and call the police, as I ran into the house and ran up the stairs to get to the baby. I walked into the room and saw the large knife near him but could not get it away from him without him seeing. I walked to the window where the man was holding the baby outstretched out of the top window. I started to talk to him and told him that he loves his baby and he would not want to harm the baby. I had to calm him down and try to bring the baby back in the room. I was talking to him for a while and he said that he and his wife were having problems, so he threatened her by putting the baby in danger. I explained that it can all be sorted by bringing the baby in as it was frightened, and we could talk about it.

After a while he did so and when he sat down to talk, the police barged through the door and grabbed the man whilst the wife grabbed the baby. They saw the large knife and looked at me. I was taken outside, and I was made to tell them what had happened. They said I was silly to go into the house especially after seeing the knife, but I said I had to do something. They agreed and I went off on my evening of drinking.

I continued with my life by going to learn Medical Studies at the Technical College. Whilst attending the course, I was doing voluntary work for an insight of medical situations. This was at the Children's Hospital where I was based on the wards, sitting with the children, bringing them toys and entertaining them and talking to worried parents and trying to reassure them by explaining medical terms whereas some doctors were not conversing to the parents in plain terms what is going on or what they are going to do, also sitting with them with a coffee and listening to their worries. I learnt a lot there about grief, medical information which backed up my college work and also how to talk to people who are lost and don't know where to turn. I was there for two years and still remember it like it was yesterday. Children are stronger than we think and know when to rest and also put a brave face on things.

There were also incidents that stick in my mind, possibly as strange happenings but also as fate.

One incident in particular was of a young boy aged about seven or eight years old. He was involved in a bad car accident when he was in his family's car. They rushed him into the A&E department to check his injuries and proceeded to give him an MRI scan. He was shown as not having any broken bones or major injuries', but an

MRI nurse noticed a mass in his brain. After more investigations it was deemed that he had an underlying brain tumour which was undetected. They quickly admitted him to the oncology ward for his cancer treatment. During my time working there I saw him on the ward for his chemotherapy visits and gradually he improved. His parents were told that if this had been undetected for any longer, then he would have gone blind as the boy didn't tell them of any symptoms that he had. If it wasn't for the car accident and finding the brain tumour due to the examination, then this would have been tragic. As I have said, sometimes bad things can turn you into another direction and change the course of your life. Life is strange.

Sometimes we have to go through painful things to make us grow stronger and mould us as a person, but the choice is to learn, accept and grow or to carry it, be resentful and angry. I was to learn that lesson myself.

I was living in a bad area, so I moved again to yet another bad area which was near my parents, we started to talk again. It was a tower block with the usual problems of parties and stabbings in the lifts on a Saturday night, it was that rough, dogs walked in pairs. I had a plank of wood in my bedroom just in case anyone decided to break into my flat in the middle of the night. I lived in that flat for five years and I had some lively moments in that block.

I was very close to my grandparents, they brought me up when I was very young, and they were by my side through troubled times. I was also close to my brother, he had strong opinions and made his thoughts well known to all. We had a fall out for a short while whilst I was going through the time when I was seventeen and had left Dave, a violent man, where I left him with just the clothes on my back. My brother had said some very nasty comments like 'you deserved it' and 'you have brought shame on our family' which neither comment was true. Since he was my brother, I forgave him, and we started talking again after a couple of months.

A while later, I had news about my uncle, who lived with my nan and grandad whilst I was living there. He brought me up on Jimi Hendrix, King Crimson and 60s rock from the age of six. When I was older, I used to go drinking with him. I heard he had cancer and was in the hospice. I went to see him with a boyfriend, and it was a picture I will never forget. He was so thin and very ill, that it was a shock to see him so close to death. News got to me a couple of weeks later that he had died. I wasn't told by my grandparents but by my mother as it was her brother. I was so upset so I went to see my grandparents and see how they were. I was met by my nan and grandad who shouted at me to get away from their home and don't come back! I was stunned and thought what has brought this on! I cried as I left their house asking them what I had done but there was no answer.

I went home and was so upset and confused. I rang my mother up on the communal phone in the tower block and she told me that they have fallen out with her too. Apparently, somebody had said something to my grandparents that was so bad and unreal that I was said to have done. I couldn't believe that they would even consider this action from me. They knew me and loved me so how could they disown me. I can only think they were misguided due to grief of losing their son and I could only imagine what they were going through. It was a bolt out of the blue and it was like a ripple in the water. It affected my close relationship with my nan and grandad, my mum's relationship with them too, and also my relatives by believing this incredible lie and fabrication. The only people who believed me were my family so because of that I lost my grandparents' relationship. It took a long time to accept this and the 'kangaroo court' action of the relatives.

I had to move on not knowing what it was really about and who said those things. I so wish I knew at the time the way I pick things up now! I collected myself and continued to see my parents and my siblings.

Life went on and I was going out with a lad at the time called Paul and had been friends with him for a while. He wrote me poetry and used to sing to me with his guitar, he was a gentle soul. I started college again and was doing Psychology and other subjects. I was so busy with my life and did not think that my periods had stopped due to anything else but the stress of my life etc. Then one day I realised I was pregnant when I went into premature labour, yes, I was slim with a bit of a tummy on me but not very big. I had a weird feeling. It may have been the day before as I was carrying very heavy library books and whilst standing for 30 minutes waiting for my bus to arrive, I felt something pull in my stomach. I got back to my flat and lay on the settee until the pain subsided. It was then I realised I was pregnant and worked out I must have been about five and a half months pregnant, the time since my last period. How could I be pregnant? the doctors said I could not have children.

I got up the next day and went to college and was in the canteen having a coffee then the pain returned, and it increased to the point where I was doubled up in agony. I was in labour and knew I had to deliver the baby myself. It was not full-term, yet I could not stop it from happening. I got myself away from people and went to the toilet whereupon I gave birth to my baby boy who was so small and clearly stillborn. I was in so much shock and I was a mess when a lady in her 50's came in and saw what distress I was in. I cleaned myself up and was given a pad and she scuttled me away to see someone else. I still don't remember much of what happened to my son as I was in shock. I should have gone to the hospital like they said but I wanted to get out of the building and get back to my flat as I was in so much pain.

I had a Doctor come out to see me and he gave me an injection to remove the placenta. I was so unwell for days that I stayed in. I was distraught at what had happened. A week or so later I went to see Paul and told him what had happened, but he didn't believe me, so I walked out of his house and never saw him again.

It took a very long time to accept losing my baby the way I did and once again the drinking ensued. It made me forget about things and I did not tell anyone about it. I saw my parents who I was starting to see again and acted as if nothing had happened. After losing my baby, I felt guilty with the what if's and if only I had not carried the heavy books the day before I lost him, for leaving him behind etc. It haunted me for years. I started to drink, and I don't mean shandy's. It was to forget about what had happened and I lost myself in that time.

I had a chance meeting with a mate called Mick who lived on the sixth floor of my tower block, I lived on the eighth floor. He had a set of tarot cards and he knew how to do readings from them. He coaxed me to listen to what he had to say in my reading. It was a promising reading, he said I would live to be elderly, I will not be alone, I will if anything be happy and will have a life of plenty. The last bits made me laugh as I was living on my own, living my life independently and living on beans on toast with a fried egg on top, of course as a staple diet as money was tight. I didn't have two brass farthings to rub together. I thanked Mick and went on my way.

This reading was to remind me of a reading I received a few years before. A gypsy man who was a true Romany and lived in a Romany caravan. He told me things which had happened already and some for the future. He said that I will have three children. He also said that having the third child will endanger my life. I jokingly said I won't have a third child then and also explained to him that I have been told by a doctor that I could not have any more children after the physical damage I received from a violent relationship. The Romany was vehement in his advice in saying there will be three children. I was to find out that, always be open to what you get told in a reading.

LIVING IN TWO WORLDS

9. *Spirit Comes Forward*

I got back into spirit work again by accident. One night I was staying at a friend's place and as I slept, I had a dream about my mother. I saw her car, which she absolutely loved, being driven fast and it then careered off the road in an area not far from my mum's house, and it crashed into the large oak tree at the bottom of the junction. I was alarmed at this as it was so real. So, for the following three nights I had the same dream, with such emotion because it was telling me that this was going to happen. My premonitions started to come back! My parents were away on holiday so I could not contact my mum and warn her of the impending car crash. I was so distracted and agitated that I could not get this out of my head until I could deliver the message.

A few days later I rang my mother and said, 'I know you love your car, but you need to sell it'. She was alarmed as she said that she too had a dream one night, whilst she was away and dreamt that she had a car crash and she saw herself bleeding in a hospital bed. I did not see this, but I saw the car and the impact but did not see who was driving it. The urgency was strong enough to tell her to sell the car. After explaining to her that I saw it three times in a row then it was going to happen. Seeing visions three times is something I came to realise; this is how I sometimes get messages of urgency especially if I have not relayed the message to the person involved. She said since I saw it three times and me being adamant that this was to happen, she decided to sell her beloved car. She said she heard it in my voice and knew it was true. She said no more after that, once the message is given it is seen as my part has been done and then the vision stops. It is in the hands of the recipient now.

A couple of weeks passed, and I went to visit my mum. It was warm and we sat in the garden. Whilst we sat and talked, she said 'I have something to tell you' I thought ok what is it? She then told me that she had sold the car to a local dealer, she handed it in to the dealer at twelve noon and about 1pm it was picked up by the new owner. He left the garage, and, on his travels, he drove down near my mum's house and he lost control of the car, he crashed into the large oak tree which is the very same spot I had seen in my visions. He was hospitalised. I was so shocked that it had happened. I thought the car being sold would stop it, but it was a lesson for me to learn that events will happen, it is just who is in the way of it happening. You cannot stop the event, but you can change some things to either lessen the blow or it is meant to be, as hard as that sounds. This crash started a chain of events that I saw and was to learn about predestined plans for all of our lives. I started to get to see, by feeling or by a warning not to go or do something. There was one time when I had left work for the day and it was evening time and I wanted to get home. I went to the local rail station and waited for my next train. It was not long before it came, and it had two carriages. I was about to get on the second carriage, the end one, and a voice came in my head that said 'No, don't get this one, get the next train'. I thought it was odd as it was getting dark soon and I wanted to get home, but I went with this message and thought ok knowing that I will have to wait another twenty or thirty minutes for the next one. I got on the next train and when we started to travel to the next station, we abruptly stopped, and we had to wait a while at the station as there was a situation on the same track up ahead. When the train guard came down to see us all, he said that the delay in carrying on with our journey was due to the previous train as it had caught fire. It was still on the tracks ahead and the passengers had to be evacuated. The train was still on the tracks abandoned. I was stunned as I realised that was what the warning was about. Once they cleared the line, we moved on and I arrived at my station a while later. I got off and went home. I put the radio on, and it mentioned that the train had caught fire and it had started in the second carriage. I thought, I am so glad I listened to my inner voice as I was warned not to go on it.

I then started taking notice of this inner voice which of course was not me but my guide who can communicate to me that way. I then used to hear the voice regarding other things and not just about warnings. I had to trust what I got told. It could be about someone's health or what they might be thinking. It was either being told, shown or feeling. Being a human being, we have to think for ourselves and sometimes we get it wrong or don't listen and this happened to me and things sometimes went a little pear shaped. You have to go with your gut instinct but also have to go by your own decisions. Sometimes we make mistakes and sometimes it works out well. I was still aware of my instincts and they were in the background. I so wanted to tell people of certain events that were to happen in their lives, but I learnt quickly that you cannot go off and tell strangers what you see, feel and get told as they will be frightened or will think you are a witch, mad or both. Also, free will is involved and people are to go by their own decisions and to live their life without my opinions put on them. I struggled with that but could not do anything about it. I still feel I want to help but I will be putting myself on them. I will only go to someone if I absolutely think it is worth the ridicule, just to make them aware of a situation which may be avoided or to know what is coming and to be ready.

Then one Christmas Eve, since I lived near my parents, I agreed for my sister to stay at my two-bedroom flat. She came to my flat in the evening and we had a few drinks and she went to bed in my spare room. About 1am in the morning a knock on the door woke me up and it was my brother, he was drunk and wanted to crash out in my flat too. I told him our sister was in the spare room so he can sleep on the settee. I went back to bed and woke the next morning to find my brother had been sick in my living room and had not cleaned it up. I went mad and asked him to clean it up which he refused to do. We were getting ourselves ready to go to our parents' house to open our presents. He got himself ready and so did my sister whilst I cleaned the mess he left behind. He was muttering under his breath and I could not understand what he was saying. He then said, 'I told them', and I said, 'You told who?' he then replied, "I told them the truth about what you had said and did, I told nan and grandad". I looked at him in disbelief and said, 'That lie, that story about me, it was you!'. He was so proud about his actions and said, 'Yes it was me' and laughed in my face and said, 'they believed me too'. I was looking at his face smirking and all I could see was a filmlike memory of the day when I saw my grandparents push me away and the relatives who shunned me and the grief of losing my grandparents, then I looked at him again smirking and laughing.

I lost it, I absolutely lost my senses. I lurched at him without thoughts in my head and felt I had to silence him. My hands were around his throat and I didn't see it or even think about it. My sister screamed at me to let go of him. She tried to get my fingers off his throat and at the end she did succeed, and I snapped out of it. It was raw anger and grief rolled into one. He ran into the bathroom and would not come out and it was a good thing he didn't!

My sister and I went to our parents and left him behind. When my mother asked where he was, my sister answered, 'He has locked himself in Kaz's bathroom to get away from her as she tried to throttle him'. That didn't go down too well especially as he was seen as the golden child and my sister did not know why I did it since she was not in the room when my brother confessed until she saw my hands around his throat.

I am a good person and have not hurt anyone before until that day, when I was pushed to my limits. It was the last time I spent Christmas Day at my parents as they said I wasn't to spend Christmas Day with them ever again. I didn't want to ruin the day any more by telling them why.

I believe sometimes we are tested during our life to make us stronger, to empathise with others, also to prepare us for what we could come across in our lives and what we are assigned to do with our lives.

10. *Time Slip*

One evening, I was walking home from a friend's house, about a mile or so from where I lived. It was starting to get a little darker but light enough to see. Everything was as it should be, cars were passing on the road and the usual noise of the living could be heard. Then when I crossed the road and arrived at the other side of the road, I noticed that it was silent. I couldn't hear the traffic as there was none. I couldn't hear anything and thought that's funny, I am not deaf. I took a couple of more steps forward and looked over to my right and saw the tree where the car accident had happened a couple of years previously with the young man who bought my mother's car. The tree was a large, old oak tree but looking at it was a shock as it was so small. I looked over and thought I will go to the bus stop, which is situated near the oak tree, to catch a bus home. As I was walking towards the bus stop, I realised that it wasn't there and in its place was a gaslight lamp stead and a man standing underneath it. He was wearing Edwardian clothing, a dark ¾ coat buttoned up and a top hat just standing still as if he was waiting for someone under the gaslight. I looked at him in disbelief and he was looking at me. He just stood there, and it took me a while to realise that I had stepped back in time as I was in a time slip. The area on one side of the road were houses from the 1930's but on the side of the road I was, on the path was different. The housing estate was gone, and it was all green grass everywhere, like it was a farm. It was eerily quiet, and I was on my own, thinking, what is going on. Since there was no bus stop and I wasn't going to walk towards the Edwardian man under the gaslight.

I carried on up the path and was bewildered by it all. I then looked ahead, and I saw a figure coming across to my left and as it came closer, I saw that it was a young lad who looked grubby with dirt on him. Blond hair, shirt sleeves were rolled up, his trousers were torn, and they stopped at his knees. He was barefooted and was walking towards me. I was shocked as he was so real looking as I could see his features and his clothes. He walked with such a direction and he knew he had to be somewhere soon. When he walked towards me, he looked straight ahead and in fact he looked through me. He looked like a stable boy, looking like he had worked hard all day, bless him. I froze and slowly walked towards him and he literally walked past me. I looked at him as he passed by my left side of me, not touching me but looking straight ahead. There was no sound of his feet and no smell of his clothes. When he walked past me, I wanted to turn around and look behind me, but my disbelief got the better of me. I wish to this day I had looked round. By now my heart was pounding and I thought 'I'm stuck and I need to get back home'.

I walked up to the top of the hill and all of a sudden, life in 1983 came back. I went to a phone box on the brow of the hill. I don't know why but I think I was questioning my sanity. I rang my mother and said, "talk to me". She said I sounded alarmed, so I explained what had happened. Since she is clairvoyant herself, she said she believed me. She told me that before the houses were built, it was a farm called Ivy House Farm as she used to get her post with the farm title in her address. That explained a lot, the farm, the stable boy but not the Edwardian man and the gaslight, unless they were from yet another era too. I started to walk home again and hoped that this was now finished. All of a sudden it went silent again. The houses had disappeared again on the other side of the road yet on my side of the road there were some modern buildings. I cautiously walked ahead and then a figure was in front of me and I couldn't make it out until she was quite close. The lady wore a black dress which puffed out from the waist. Her hair was tied back as in a bun and she looked mournful. Her expression was of a strong woman who looked sad and in thought. She looked at me and knew I was there. Her eyes acknowledged me. As we got closer, she looked at me and then went off the path at an angle. As she turned, she turned her head and looked at me, but she didn't speak. Whilst I was taking this all in, she walked through the brick wall and disappeared from view. I was only a few steps away from her and I looked at the brick wall and there was no entry. She simply went through it. By then I thought I am going home now and not stopping for anything.

I ran the 1½ miles to my flat and locked my door. I laugh to myself now about this as spirit cannot be kept out if they wish to contact you. I had no understanding then of what had happened nor of spirit's ways of communication.

After this, I was made aware of a Clairvoyant/Medium called David Starkey who had an office in the City Centre. One evening I went to see him to get clarity and answers of what has been happening to me. As soon as I walked through the door, he stopped me in my tracks by saying 'you are a Clairvoyant'. I had not spoken to him yet nor sat down. I looked at him and he said 'you have had this gift since you were a child'. I was surprised that he could tell me straight away that the events I had been having were real. He was so good at explaining about the senses, clairvoyance - clear seeing, clairaudience – clear hearing, clairsentience – clear feeling, and Claircognizance – clear knowing but I was to learn the other senses, clairgustance – clear tasting, clairalience – clear smelling and Clairtangency – clear touching which is called psychometry and it was something that I came to use some years later. It all made sense to me, no pun intended, as a child with this gift and no explanations. You feel like you are going mad but now I had a better understanding of things.

I got on with my life and accepted that spirit was part of my life. I went out and socialised and sometimes I picked up on certain people's energy. I was not purposely looking into someone's life, but it came to me and I later learnt that it was their aura I was picking up on. I didn't always listen to my intuition though which is a human fault. I also felt as though I was not alone and being watched over. I was in and out of relationships as I was too independent and did not suffer fools gladly.

LIVING IN TWO WORLDS

11. *New Start*

After what had happened to me a few years previously, it made me realise that I will not put up with violence nor controlling behaviour. I went to college part time studying Law/Criminal Law and Psychology and also worked at the Citizens Advice Bureau. It was where it helped me to think on my feet. I was trained up by the manager and was ready for the public. I went to different places to see people to give them advice on a lot of subjects. Some of the cases I saw will always stay in my mind. One day I would be at a psychiatric hospital talking to the patients who needed benefits advice or legal advice. Some of the cases I saw will always stay in my mind, such as the female patient at the psychiatric hospital who was there because her sons were beating her up and taking her money. Due to this behaviour she had a breakdown. Once she felt better with medication for her nerves and counselling from the staff, I arranged for the local housing authority to rehouse her in an area that she felt safe and that her sons could not find her.

Another day was a secure male prison called Winson Green prison in Birmingham, where I gave advice to the families of the prisoner and also to the prisoner in his cell, where a prison officer stood outside the cell. I was fine with this as I was studying Criminal Law and I wanted actual practical work in this field as I was hoping to get a place in Aston University for my LLB Law degree. It was impartial work, I told them do not tell me what you have done or accused of and they were fine with that.This did not go to plan with one mother in the family unit who came to see me.

She came for advice for her son who was in prison and I relayed the advice that I could do and look into. She then broke my rule, she started telling me what her son was accused of and was shouting that he was innocent and he was angelic. The more she told me, the more I remembered the crime. He was accused of raping a woman in a multi storey car park, apparently, he was in his car and watched her walk to hers. He then attacked her, raped her then he stabbed her multiple times. The part I will never forget is where people heard her screams and ran and stood beside her as she lay on the ground bleeding and slipping away, he was kneeling next to her trying to 'comfort her', it was said that some of the people had heard her say 'he did it' over and over again, until she died. He was arrested there and then as luckily some people heard her voice pleading with them. I believe they did a citizen's arrest whilst the police came. The local newspapers printed the story giving the full details which was upsetting. I listened whilst this was going around in my head, and then she left the room protesting his innocence. Seconds later, I had a woman come into the room to see me shouting 'Do you know who she is, her son is a monster', " why did you talk to her?" I had to calm the woman down and explain that I cannot pass comments on any cases or crimes as I have to be impartial. It doesn't mean I do not have my personal thoughts. I told her that I was doing my job and if I passed judgement on any person in the prison then I could not do my job properly. She understood.

It did leave its mark on me though. I wanted to be a solicitor, but could I defend someone who did such a heinous crime? I carried on with my Law/Criminal Law and Psychology studies.

Another day I was at Dr Barnardo's with social workers and abused children. It made me see the world in all walks of life and compassion grew from there. One visit to the Dr Barnardo's centre where I worked was a very upsetting situation. In one room was a child who was too scared to return to his parents, who were sitting in another room waiting for him. The problem was that he had been taken away from his parents and fostered to another family due to the injuries he had received in his parents' care. I saw the photos of the burns and extensive bruises that the child had endured which was horrendous. He was happy with the foster family, but a Judge had deemed the parents had learnt the error of their ways and said that he should go back to his parents. He was too frightened and would not leave the safety of his room with the social worker and myself. I went with the social worker as she had to take the boy into the room where his parents were, under duress. The parents were getting annoyed at this and were calling him to go to them. It was awful to see. The social workers were so professional and knew they had to do this as it was instructed by law but once the parents left the centre with their son, one social worker was in tears as she had seen this all too often. They were there to protect the children, yet the law let them down. I also saw people enduring hardship, debt, no food, loss of family members and all manner of life changing decisions. This was a time in my life where I knew I was to help people with my best abilities now and in the future.

In the Citizens Advice Bureau office, a woman was being shielded and protected in our office as her husband was outside threatening to hurt her when she left our building. I saw the Q.C. (Queen's Counsel to the courts) who resided in our building, and he gave me a letter to give to the judge at the nearby Magistrates Court. The letter was to obtain a court injunction to keep the husband away from the estranged wife and if he comes within five miles of her home or near her then he will be arrested. I ran through the back door, ran to the courts, obtained the injunction and ran to the back door as the front door was locked to stop the abusive husband getting in as he was threatening the staff to get to his wife. I then got let in before he saw me, thank god. The Q.C signed the form and then I went with him to serve it to the husband at the front door. The husband was ranting and raving, calling his wife to come out, she was still frightened and stayed in the office, then the police arrived, and he scarpered. Once the wife had got the courage to leave with the police then they would have escorted her to her home and assumed her husband lived elsewhere.

I was in a relationship with someone who had a different childhood to me and was from a steady family background. During our courtship, I started having more visits from spirit. Many times, I felt these visitations in my flat. One time I was in my flat and it was about 1pm in the afternoon, I felt a presence who tried to talk to me but I was getting frustrated as I could not hear what they were saying with my ears and had asked them to show me as a film in my head so I could see what they are saying. All of a sudden, I got it, it was a message to say that my boyfriend's stepfather was going to pass away soon as he had asbestosis and had been ill for a few months. I had to tell him this message, which was not believed at the time. I gave my message and that is all I can do. It is up to the recipient to accept it and see what unfolds or not believe what has been given to them. I did not go to the boyfriend's house as I did not see eye to eye with his stepdad even before he was ill, so I stayed at my flat.

I loved my flat on the eighth floor of a sixteenth storey block as once I closed my front door, it was my sanctuary. There were stabbings in the lift most Saturday nights. You walked in the lift on the Sunday morning to go to the shops for your paper and cigarettes and sure enough there was blood everywhere. The kids used to set fire to the large communal bin's, so we had to be evacuated a few times. The one time that I was personally evacuated was when a fireman knocked on my door one evening and said to 'get out as there was a fire in the flat above mine and water will be seeping through my electrics'. It was drug addicts that had set fire to a mattress in the living room above mine.

I was broken into once on Friday 13th, I got to my front door and it had been crowbarred in. I had to do something as I was not sure if they were still in the flat and how many there were! I started to walk into my flat shouting "I'm coming in, so you had better get out". As soon as I said that, I noticed that a few of my things were put in piles in the hallway. I walked through to the living room thinking they will be in there and no sign of them. Then it hit me, they must have been disturbed or realised that I had nothing of value. After that I kept a big piece of wood in my bedroom as that was the first room near the front door and if anyone came in whilst I was in then I would protect myself and they would be limping out of my flat. Because of those incidents, you had to have a survival instinct about yourself. There was always some form of activity in the block of flats where I was.

Anyway, I carried on as per usual until the week after my message. I came home one afternoon to find a note on my hall floor, and it was from my boyfriend Don. It said that his stepdad Lee had died the night before. I looked at the kitchen clock and it was 1pm in the afternoon and it was seven days from the exact time and to the day that I gave the message to Don about Lee. I couldn't believe it and the message was correct.

I went to the funeral as awkward as it was and went for Don's sake. Gradually I got to know his mum properly. She was a churchgoer and did not agree with my way of life especially with the spirit world. I started to stay at her house where her late husband had died. A few weeks after the funeral, I slept in a spare bedroom and suddenly awoke in the night, to someone looking straight at me from the bottom of the bed. I could make out it was a man who looked at me as if to say, 'what are you doing here?' I recognised that it was Lee, Don's stepdad. He was real and large as life. As soon as I sat up in bed to talk to him, he disappeared in front of me. He was letting me know that this was his house. I didn't tell anyone the next day as I did not want to upset the family. This was not to be the last time I saw Lee in the house.

I stayed most Saturday nights at his mum's house. One evening I went upstairs to go to the bathroom. As soon as I left the bathroom, I felt the energy change. I started to walk across the landing when my exit was blocked by Lee. He stood there in my way letting me know it is his house. I stood there and spoke to him. I said firmly 'I know this is your house, but I am a guest here'. He looked at me knowing I could see him and then he disappeared. I went downstairs and felt compelled this time to tell don and his mum. They were shocked and obviously non-belief came into their thoughts. I thought that they know now, and nothing was said about it. A few months later it happened again, Lee was on the landing and I told him 'I know you are here to protect the family. I understand that, but I am looking after them too and I am not a threat'. He looked at me and then he walked to the side of the landing and let me pass.

This was to be the last time I saw Lee.

LIVING IN TWO WORLDS

12. Sid

I still popped into see my neighbour in my tower block. His name was Sid and he lived alone. I used to go around to his flat most days to see if he was alright and watch the telly with him and make cups of tea, chat about the war and companionship for both of us! He was a strong, independent man in his mid 70s. He went to the shops on his own as he liked it that way and put money on the horses as he loved his betting and he was good at it too. He had his own system as he used to write down the names of the horses that were the winners and runners-up for all the races in this country. When he wanted to put some bets on, he would consult his 'oracles', his books. He had been doing it for some time because he had a couple of books with results of previous races on etc. He won and of course lost some but that was the game he wanted to play. If he watched the race on the telly, then he would shout at the telly and laugh if he won and get exasperated if he lost. Then it was 'make him a cup of tea-time'. He was a good man, no nonsense person. When he had had enough of your company you knew. I would go back to my flat. I knew he had a story to tell about his life.

One day he told me what it was. He was engaged during the WWII period, and when he went to war with the troops, his fiancée worked in the ammunition's factory on the Coventry Road in Birmingham. During the war the German planes flew over the Midlands and bombed Coventry Cathedral and a lot of Birmingham due to the assets that we could give to our troops. They wanted to stop production of ammunition and weapons etc in our factories. Unfortunately, they targeted the factory that Sid's fiancée worked in and it was her shift to work that day. They bombed it and razed it to the ground. I don't know if any workers survived but I know that Sid's fiancée didn't. He did not know this and when he came back from the war, surviving what he went through to make a life with her. It was all in vain in his eyes, he found out she had been killed and it devastated him to the core. It actually changed him as a person. He made his mind up to live a solitary life and not get close to anyone and certainly not be with or love another woman again as she would not compare to his fiancée and he could love no one like he loved her. It made him an independent person with low tolerance of people but when you got in between his ribs, he accepted you. I believe to this day that we were mates.

One day I got up early as usual, but I had the feeling that something was not right. I knocked on Sid's door and there was no answer as he used to either leave the door on the latch or yell 'it's open'. I knew something was odd as he was an early riser too. I opened the letter box flap and shouted 'Sid' and all of a sudden, I could hear a faint 'help me'. I felt sick, I thought, where is he? I shouted back and tried to find out where he was, and he told me he was on the kitchen floor. I shouted, 'hang in there, I'm going to get help'. I ran to the phone box on the sixth floor and rang 999, not knowing what to say as I did not know what state Sid would be in. I said he has collapsed, and he is on the floor of his flat, and was told the ambulance was on its way. I ran upstairs and shouldered the front door as best as I could, but to no avail. I asked one of the neighbours to help me barge the door open. The man helped and I ran to the kitchen and found Sid on the floor, struggling to speak. I spoke to him as I was kneeling on the floor next to him, and stroked his hair to calm him down, and told him that the ambulance is on its way. I knew I couldn't move him, but I was not a first aider so did not know what to do other than comfort him. He was frightened and upset as he was proud and did not want to be found like this. The ambulance came and took him away, saying to me that he may have had a stroke. I didn't know his sister's phone number, but he told the hospital staff where to contact her. Sid was in hospital for a while and got himself discharged as he wanted to be back in his flat. I was not surprised as he wanted his familiar surroundings.

He settled back in and I went around often to see him. His speech was not so good and his right side (his dominant side) was not as it should have been. He had trouble holding things and got frustrated. He would not l let you do anything for him unless I saw him struggle and then I took over. I think we understood each other with time, he got back on his feet and started to go out shopping again, putting bets on had kept him going.

One winter though, he went out early and I got a knock on my door from one of my neighbours to say that Sid had fallen on ice and cracked his head which was bleeding. Someone found him outside the tower block and got him rushed to hospital. He got better again but this was the last time he was my neighbour. Social Services had rehoused him into a low-rise block for elderly people. He was not happy about this. I visited him often and we talked about his life and the outside world. One day I was combing his hair and found a hole in his skull. He pulled my hand away and when I pushed him for a reason for the hole, he said he was shot in the war and he did not want to talk about it and that was the last time I asked him.

During this time, I was engaged to be married, so I visited less and less because Sid was getting a bit fractious about me getting married, and he felt that he was being abandoned again. I tried to explain to him that I will see him, but he wasn't having any of it. We were mates, I was twenty-five, and I had to live my life. It was a shame that he felt that way, deep down he was lonely. His sister came around a couple of times a week and I explained to her that I could not come around as much. It was to be the last time I saw him alive.

Years later I went to look him up on the electoral rolls in Birmingham Library. He had moved into a home near his sister. He had died 9 years after I had last seen him. I found out where he was buried and one day, I went to see his grave. It was such a large cemetery, I knew roughly which section he was in, but I could not find it. Then I said to Sid, 'give me a sign where you are please'. I looked ahead and I saw in the corner of my eye, a white feather floating to the left of me, a couple of rows back. I walked over to see where it had landed, and it was next to his grave. He was buried in the same plot as his mother. I arranged some flowers in the pot and had a quick chat with him, hoping he was listening. I turned to go and sure enough I saw his figure standing near a tree at least 15 feet away from me. I smiled and thanked him for showing me his grave and I sent him my love and wishes. That was the last time I went to his grave.

Signs are everywhere, you just need to ask for help. A few years before, I was looking for a grave and I asked spirit for help locating it. I saw on the right-hand side of the cemetery, a balloon bobbing up and down on a calm day, no wind at all. I thought that's strange. I made my way to the balloon which was attached to a headstone and the grave I wanted to find was right next to it. Once again, I thanked spirit for their help.

Sometimes we have signs appear to us and we don't take heed of them when we should do as I was to find out soon.

13. *I Did Not Listen*

My wedding day was going to be eventful, it comes in threes, so they say, that was true that day. A little event went wrong early in the day, but the main event was when after my instinct told me not to go ahead with this marriage, even my dad said in the wedding car on the way to the church said 'you don't have to do this Kaz, you can go back home'.

We even went around the church green three times to make my mind up. I wasn't listening to my instinct, nor my dad and went into the church. No sooner had I got to the front of the church where the vicar was waiting, he says to us all, 'This is a thirteenth century church so before I proceed with this wedding, I will ask you to dig deep into your pockets and give donations of money into the buckets which can be found near the door, this is for our roof appeal'. He talked about the state of the roof of the church and how much is needed etc. I was a bit surprised, but I thought it was fair enough for a good cause.

Back to the wedding service he started to read the vows and when he got to the bit about any persons who believe this marriage should not go ahead then speak up now. It went silent in the church and then a bang, it was pitch black. I couldn't see a thing. I heard my side of the church where family and friends were sitting say 'someone put 50p in the meter' and then I said 'who am I marrying here' as I grasped someone's hand hopefully not the vicar's. People were laughing and I thought what a thing to happen. That was a warning from spirit to get out, which I didn't take heed to. The service carried on in the dark and I wasn't sure if the vicar was getting married to me, the best man or don. Once the ceremony was done, Don and I had to go to another part of the church which was near a window where we were relying on the sunny August afternoon which was well lit for us to sign the register after seeing it was Don I had married. My wedding photos are showing us in the dark getting married and then in the light signing the register. When we came out of the church in the dark to a very sunny outside, I saw the next bride and groom to be married waiting patiently as they had been told that they could not go in to the church as it is dark and it was not fair to the couple, especially the entrance of the bride would not have being seen.

My reception went wrong too, and my guests thought the lights going out at the service at the apt moment was a stunt we had set up, like I wanted to get married in the dark. I do laugh at that thought! I think it was a big warning as I was not listening to my instinct.

Well married life went on its way and no sooner had we got married, I found out I had Endometriosis which when explained made sense of the abdominal pains I was having every day.

I had to have surgery to remove what they could and to sew my womb to the inside of my abdominal wall as the damage Dave had done years ago had kicked under my bowel. I was told that I will have no children as the damage was so bad.

I told my Sister in law called Jackie, who I am still very close to. She knew how damaged I was inside, this was due to Dave's violence and the Endometriosis. I used to see her a lot and she was having a time of it with my brother, in their marriage. They had my nephew and my brother was shirking his responsibilities in the marriage and as a parent. She single handedly brought him up and she is such a strong woman. On one of my visits she told me that she would have a baby for me, if that could be done. I was overwhelmed by this as I could not agree for her to do that. I hugged her and told her that if I am not meant to have them then so be it. Don, my husband, did not want to adopt either as he felt that the baby would not be his, and not coming from his efforts.

A couple of years later I was told that I was to have a hysterectomy, to rid myself of the Endometriosis. It was February when I went to the hospital for my usual appointment there and was told that I am booked in for the hysterectomy in June. Whilst I was there, I asked the doctor to check if I was pregnant as I was feeling a bit rough and could not stand the smell of coffee. He said to me 'you cannot be pregnant' but he humoured me with my wee sample. He came back and said I need to sit down and said, 'we are not taking your bits out as someone else needs them'. I was shocked and happy at the same time. I told Don, family and friends and it was a miracle. Nat was called a miracle baby by the doctors and nurses. I had a rough time with the pregnancy as I was carrying my baby in an awkward way, as the surgeons had previously sewn the womb to the inner wall of my abdomen, painful as it was. I had Endometriosis so severe that it would be a miracle to conceive, let alone carry the baby to full term. I was also attending Cardiac clinic as my heart was struggling with the pregnancy. A few stays in the hospital during the pregnancy put paid to that!

When a woman is in labour, why do some men do daft things.I went into labour on my own at home, and Don came home to see me struggling. He got me to the hospital car park and as I got out of the car, I shouted 'It's coming'. A male porter standing at the main doors says, 'Do you want a wheelchair?', and I said sarcastically 'oh no, I will just walk into the hospital what do you think!!' as I'm nearly on my knees. The baby was ready, no mistake. I got into the hospital and a monitor was placed on my heart and on the baby's head as she was not coming out as she wanted.

After being in strong labour for about six hours, I had asked for an epidural whereupon my husband says 'you said you were planning not to have one', and I said in a strained voice, 'I didn't know I was going to be in strong labour for this long with no pain relief', also it was on the lines of get it me now please. I got it thank god. Don went home as he was tired, and I was alone. Three hours later when a midwife came to see me, she noticed that my heart and the baby's heart was in distress and I was told by a doctor that I needed an emergency caesarean now. Don then walked in on cue. Since Don had to sign the consent forms, he was being indecisive about signing them. The Doctor made his mind up for him by saying 'you sign the form now or you will lose your wife and your baby'. Enough said!

I was awake for the caesarean and saw them take away my daughter for a while as she was blue and lifeless. They looked after her and she was given to me a few hours later. I stayed in hospital for a week and realised I had a baby that had a lot to say. I was woken up in the night by the nurse saying to me 'Can you please get your baby from the nursery as she won't stop screaming and she is keeping the other babies awake'. Oops, I shuffled down the corridor to get her.

I eventually went home seven days later, and we got on with our lives and I went back to work when she was less than a year old due to financial restraints. Jackie kindly offered to have Nat in the daytime whilst I was at work. She said since she had Ben to look after and one more will be no problem, it was her niece. I will always be grateful to her for the gesture as it helped so much. I don't think she will ever know how much she did for Nat and myself. Don would drop Nat off early in the morning and either myself or Don would pick her up after work.

One morning she was in her cot and as I was about to open her bedroom door, I heard a female voice in her room saying, 'Oh Natalie', very softly and endearing. I was very surprised by this. It was spirit and it was someone looking over her. I did not go in until the voice had gone and she was wide awake. One time I felt the lady who used to live in the flat who had passed away, and I would often smell Devon Violets perfume in our bedroom, also I would feel her presence in the flat.

When Natalie was about two years old, we were both in the living room and Natalie turned around to me and said, 'lady in the corner'. I thought she saw her too! She has the ability and it has been passed down to her through my lineage.

When Natalie was three, Don and I had split up and I was a single parent for a while. Due to me not being able to drive, I took Nat to a nursery not far from where I lived, as I could not get to Jackie's at 7am as my work started at 8am. Full time hours and long days, but it had to be done.

One day I got a phone call from her nursery to say that Natalie was not well, and could I please pick her up. I left work and collected her, I got a lift in a friend's car and as we were at a junction to turn right to go home, a voice said to me to turn left and go straight to the hospital. I did as I was instructed as I sometimes did with spirit. By the time I got there, she was drowsy and not well at all. She was put in a bed on a ward and a female doctor said she will be alright as she is just dehydrated due to her being sick. I knew it was more serious than that as she was fading fast and her eyes were rolling back into her head. I couldn't sit there and watch this.

I ran down the ward and found a male doctor and told him that my daughter is in a bad way. He went to see her and with one look at her he knew he had to act quickly. He lay her down on the bed and then started to feel her tummy very gently. He then pushed hard on her stomach twice with such force that upset me. He then said that he felt something pop inside. He then asked which doctor told me she was ok and just dehydrated, when he found her, he called her and then he tore a strip off her verbally. He shouted, 'did you not see this? did you not know?', pointing to Natalie's stomach. The next thing the male doctor grabbed the bed and the female doctor grabbed the other end and both ran down the corridor with me in tow all the way to the ultrasound department. He said that if what he has done has not worked then Natalie will have to go to the Children's Hospital by helicopter as she has about thirty minutes left to live. I couldn't take it in, and I was beside myself.

They scanned her and it seems that what he had done had worked. Thank god, what had happened was her bowel had telescoped itself into the other half of her bowel and the toxins in the trapped part was poisoning her body. She was going to be alright, he told me. I thanked him for saving her life, yet I felt I could not have thanked him enough as he took it in his stride.

She was in the hospital for a week and I slept next to her on the ward on a makeshift bed for the first few nights. I realised I could have lost her. A while later I started a relationship with Peter who I had known as friends. He was older than me and had older children, and he was good to Natalie. We lived together for a while and then incidents of young children were being taken from their gardens and bundled into a car by two adults. I felt that Birmingham was not a safe place for a young child to play out etc.

14. *New Home*

We decided to move to Wales where it was rural and safe for children to play out. I absolutely loved living there with farms behind our house, sitting in the garden hearing sheep bleating, children were safe, and neighbours watched over all the children in the play areas near their homes. It was a quiet and small market town which had a feeling of everyone knowing everyone else's business or they thought they did. I used to go to Natalie's school sports days which was fun to watch. I felt we had found a place to call home which protected us from the harshness of the city.

She was a natural swimmer, so she was entered into the 'Urdd' Youth Championships for her school and county. She did well there, she had a lot of friends and she would walk safely to the shops on her own or take our border collie for a walk near the farms. It seems that spirit was never far away though. The one day a friend of Natalie's was in our house and all of a sudden, I heard a scream. I ran to where they were, and Natalie was excited, but her friend was absolutely scared. They both said they had seen a man in solid form in a leather jacket walk past them on the landing. I was aware that there was a man in the house, but I did not see him like they did. Natalie was accepting of this, but her friend was not happy, and she very rarely came around to our house again. Natalie became more aware of spirit, the older she got, but she did not understand how others could not see them or were scared of them.

I was still getting visions and premonitions. I was at work one day and was sitting next to a girl called Dawn. We used to chat in between telephone calls as we worked in a call centre. I was talking to her and all of a sudden I saw in front of me a vision, like watching a film of her being pregnant and then seeing her with a red haired baby sitting on a blanket, he was chunky looking and they were sitting near a riverside with another lady. I told her what I had seen and she said that it could not be her as she and her husband cannot have children. She called her husband Jaffa as he is seedless. I told her all the details and she said she will take it in, but it won't happen. I left the job for another and after a few months I went back to the call centre job. I saw dawn again and she was pregnant. She said she couldn't believe it, so I said, 'I told you' and laughed. I asked her if she remembered what else I had told her, and she said she had remembered.

Dawn left the company to have her baby and one day I was shopping and I had happened to see Dawn pushing a pushchair with her husband. I said hello and looked at the baby, it was a boy and he had such red hair and he was chunky too. Dawn and her husband had dark brown hair so they could not understand why their son's hair was red. We were talking and all of a sudden dawn chirps to me with 'Do you remember your vision of me being on a blanket near the riverside with my baby, well it came true as my sister and I had a picnic the other day next to the River Severn in the town and we were on the blanket you described'. I was surprised but pleased that my vision came true especially about their baby.

I left that job again and started to work in an Accounts role which was not a job I would have chosen but it was one I fell into at the right time. It was the same workplace as Peter. It was a good job and I made friends quite quickly. I still speak to the girls from time to time. We used to go out for drinks and pub quizzes etc. I also kept in touch with a girl I worked with in my previous job. She came from Birmingham too and her daughter was Nat's age and they both went to the local school together, they were best mates. My friend knew I saw spirit and got premonitions and although she thought it strange, she accepted that it was what I was about. I started to sit in a Spiritual Circle at the Spiritual Centre on a Saturday afternoon with another friend called Sara who lived in the same road as me. She had two girls that played with Nat too. I used to watch the Medium's demonstrate as I was in awe of them. So in one class I attended, we were asked to put an item of ours on a tray and the tray was given to the medium to choose an item to hold so she could do a reading by picking up the energy of the owner, this is called Psychometry.

During the afternoon session she picked up my item and said some things which would be applicable for a later time and not the present. I accepted this gracefully and she moved on to another person. At the end of the session I went to see the medium and Sara was with me. I started to say thank you for the reading and all of a sudden, my mouth opened and what fell out surprised me. I said to her 'you were in Bearwood recently', I got told by a voice and I also saw her in a vision shopping in a street there. I thought oh my god what did I say that to her for! She looked at me stunned and said "yes I was in Bearwood yesterday, how did you know that? Bearing in mind that I live in Wales and Bearwood is a place in the West Midlands. I wasn't there and she was asking me about my visions, so I told her about them, and she said that I should use my gifts and also try Psychometry, which is what she had done that afternoon. I thought I would give it a go at some time to see if I could pick up energy from an item regardless if the owner is alive or passed over, even though I thought I can't do that! The medium said that I could do it, and I explained that I would like to help people on both sides of this world. I said goodbye and Sara and I were talking about the session and she said, 'you heard what she said, try and use your abilities'. I thought about it and left it at that.

I got on with my life as usual but continued to attend the

Spiritual Circle. One morning when Nat and I were eating our breakfast in the living room, I felt a presence pass us both in the room and this then became a regular appearance at a certain time as I looked at the clock on the mantelpiece. One day I looked at the clock on the mantelpiece and thought I would get up a minute earlier before the usual time and I started to slowly walk down the stairs as this was an upside-down house and the living room was on the top floor. As soon as I got about halfway down the stairs, I turned around and I saw something I will never forget, and I know what I saw. I glimpsed a glowing female figure in white floating across the landing and she saw me look at her. She was interacting with me and she was angelic looking. I still believe to this day that she was an angel. I said hello and told her that I was honoured to see her. She glided across the top of the stairs looking at me and then she continued into the living room where Nat was sitting. That angelic being was the energy that I felt every morning passing us at the same time. She did not appear again in that house, but I felt that what had happened was so special.

I continued to attend the circle classes and I met a lovely girl called Cerys, she was so gifted, and she told me a lot about her gifts. She told me that you choose your family before you are born and the group of people close to you are people you have been together with in a previous life. I was mind boggled on that fact. She told me that her son was her father in a previous life. She proceeded to tell me

121

what he had done in his life and how he died. I am open minded, but I thought I have some learning to do on this subject. I was aware of Reincarnation especially when I told my mother and sister that they were not my family and I did not understand why I was there and this was when I was young, but this to me was a step further. I took her at her word and I took it on board, the thing is in years to come I was to hear this revelation again and again!

I had been living in Wales for a couple of years or so and was settled, then one night I was alarmed by a dream/vision I had. It was a Monday night and I stayed awake thinking about what I had seen, not sure if it was a nightmare or an actual premonition. It was of a teenage girl of school age who looked scared and she was in a wooded area. I felt it was mid-morning and she looked rather dazed, but it was what she said in her head, I could hear her thoughts. She said, 'he is going to kill me'. Her eyes were wide now and all of a sudden, I saw the hole in the ground where she was placed, and he hit her across the head with a shovel a couple of times. She fell lower into the hole and he was satisfied that she would not tell anyone what had happened. I was shocked and upset and also thought why, who and where is this. I lay in bed trying to get my head around it. I thought this a bad dream and tried to get back to sleep.

No sooner had I settled down again, I saw her again. She

was walking down the street in the early morning with her school friends as this was a normal day for her. All of a sudden, a van pulls up and the man says hello to her and her schoolmates who are all young girls. The girls know he is confident, and he likes young girls, but she knows him very well. I got the impression that he gave her lifts in his van, so it seemed nothing was unusual about this. Then it all changed, and he went to a DIY store and bought some goods. I feel she is in the van waiting for him. Then it jumps to him pulling up at a beauty spot, He goes to the back of the van and that is when I see what he is wearing. Denim jeans, work boots and very scruffy looking. He opens the back doors of the van and I see he has building equipment, tools etc in his van. He reaches for a spade/shovel and then it takes me to the spot where he digs the hole. He walks her through the woods, and she is groggy and not really with it, almost to the point of being drugged. She is placed in the hole and starts to come around, a bit and sees him and realises what he is about to do. It then fast forwards to him going home. He has personal items of hers and they were scrunched up in his hand and he hurriedly puts them under the sink for quickness, hoping they don't get found by his wife! I saw most of the story and felt it was too real to be a bad dream.

A couple of days later, I went to Sara's house for a cup of tea, and a chat. I don't buy newspapers, but Sara had one, so I just picked it up and browsed through it whilst she was washing up. Within a few pages I was stopped in my tracks, I came across a photo of the girl I had seen the other night. The headlines said she was missing. I shouted to Sara 'I saw this girl in a dream the other night, I saw what happened'. Sara said, 'Are you sure it's her?' whereupon I said I was positive. I remember her face; she was a schoolgirl. I told Sara that I needed to tell someone about the man and what I had seen that had happened to her. The article said to ring a certain police authority for that area. I thought if I ring the police, they won't believe me, it's not like the police in America who listen to psychics/mediums for help on missing people. Also, the missing girl lived in the South of England and I was in Wales, all the more they will not believe me.

I went home and rang the constabulary in that area as they were appealing for information. I spoke to a policeman at the station who once I started to mention that I lived in Wales and tried to tell him what I had seen in my vision, he then called me a 'crank' and 'I know what type of people you are'. I was really shocked at his opinion of me and then he put the phone down on me. I sat still for a while, thinking what can I do. I must remember the details of what I had seen. A couple of days passed by and I thought this is no good, I have got to tell them what I had seen. I rang again and this time it was a policewoman who answered. As soon as she answered I said, 'please hear me out before you put the phone down like your colleague did the other day, I don't care what you think I am but just take the details down'. She said she would. After the phone call I could not stop thinking about the girl and said to the heavens that I had done my best to help her and her family. A couple of days later it was announced on the news that a man was helping the police with their enquiries. I was relieved and thought thank god this will be sorted out now and he will tell them where she was and confess his crime.

It went quiet though and then a while later in the news it was announced that they had arrested a man. The details were like I had said, he was a builder, the van, what he wore and also, she did know him well. What came to light was horrendous though, he also would not tell the police nor her family where she was, but they knew she was not alive anymore. I feel so much for the family as he did not give them closure, he refused to tell them where she was. I have tried to find the location of the beauty spot that I saw. I tried to tell the policewoman the area I saw but they still don't know where this was. I was glad they got him, and he went to court and was found guilty and he was given a life sentence, but this won't bring her back. After this event it made me want to listen to spirit communication and try and help the ones who have passed on and are lost.

Years ago, when I lived in Birmingham, once again I saw a vision of a young woman who was abducted after meeting a man whom she was meant to show around a house, as she did this as a job. The client had taken her to an area which was derelict. It looked like an old army barracks or an old building in the middle of nowhere. He kept her there blindfolded and she was huddled in a corner, yet with her I could not see where she was killed. There is a man in prison for another abduction and murder and I believe that this is him as he looks like the man I saw. She too has not been found and he will not tell the family where she is. I did not say anything to anyone as I did not have any information where she could be found etc. I have accepted that I do get visions and also visits from spirits asking for help. I would write things down so I would remember and for future confirmations.

I had to get on with my life again and it seemed the nightly visits were affecting my health. I wasn't sleeping well, and, in the daytime, it seemed I was 'switched on' all the time. I could see spirit and hear them. I eventually made myself go to a spiritualist church and met a brilliant medium there. She told me I was open to spirit and needed to close down when I went to bed and in certain times of the day especially at work. I said that I didn't know how to, so she explained to me about the chakras and the crown chakra, through visualisations how to open and close this when I am busy and need to sleep. It was very helpful. I did the technique she showed me, and I slept a little better.

15. The Reveal

One evening I was washing up at the sink and was aware that someone was behind me. I turned around and to my surprise there was a Chinese man. He wore black tunic and trousers with an oriental hat and his hair was long and in one plait. I looked at him for what seemed like seconds, he was smiling and then disappeared. I thought who that was and then I carried on as normal. A few days later I visited the medium I had seen at the church and she turned around to me and said, 'you have seen your guide', I said 'my guide, I didn't know I had one'. She said, 'he is Chinese' and she described him exactly. I was pleasantly surprised at this as I now know who he was. I asked about my guide and what do they do?. She told me that he was here to help and advise me on my now spiritual path. Guides can only advise if asked as our life is governed by free will. They cannot interfere unless necessary. This was comforting to know, and she also said, 'you have a guide who brought you into this world and stays with you and then takes you over to the other side when it is time'. You also have guides who 'turn up' when a certain event or help is needed. They are all different but act as an aid on your spirit path. I was so fascinated, I couldn't wait to see my Chinese guide again, but this did not happen. I came across different guides instead and still do. I thanked the medium for her help and her teachings. It is something I will treasure. I still had subtle warnings of events that are to happen.

I was at work and talking to my boss and all of a sudden, I could smell flowers. I thought ok, I normally get that when someone is going to pass over. I said to him 'can you smell flowers?' just to clarify it was not my imagination, and he flatly said No! I thought about this and said in my head, 'who is this for?' and was shown a picture of a lovely lady who worked at our place as a cleaner who I had spoken to earlier that week. I said to my boss 'don't worry about it' and I walked off. Sure enough a few days later, I got told that the lady I saw had in fact died the night before. She was a lovely soul. I went to her funeral and said my goodbyes to her knowing that she was in a good place already. I still have feelings about people etc.

A while later, I was told that my Nan was in hospital. She had had three strokes and was now unable to talk. I knew I had to see her as I had not seen her or spoke to her since the incident years ago. I made the trip from Wales to Birmingham; it was hard to see her lying in the bed. She saw me and she turned away, so I realised that she did not know that I was innocent of what I was accused of. I looked her in the face and said, 'I have come all the way from Wales to see you and I am not leaving here until you look at me'. She turned around and looked at me and then she smiled at me as best as she could. She tried to put her hand out to me, and I bent over and kissed her on the forehead as she was so ill and frail. She whispered, 'I'm sorry and I love you', I said that it was alright. I sat and spoke to her and she could not speak as it had taken her voice, but her eyes smiled. My Granddad came into the room and he hugged me. He said he missed me and that he was sorry, and I said that it was ok. This was not the time to hold onto the anger of all the years without them. After chatting and hugging, I left to go home. I saw my Nan one more time and it was like 'coming home again'.

Then one evening I was in the garden and all of a sudden, I felt a great wave of emotion, sadness and with a knowing. I told Peter 'my nan is dying, I have to ring the hospital'. It was so strong! I rang the hospital and spoke to the male nurse and I said, "my nan is dying isn't she, she hasn't long". He was shocked that I said that as he told me that he was about to ring my grandad and tell him to get to the hospital quickly as she was dying. He asked me how I knew, so I said that I saw it and I knew but of course he didn't understand. I was so upset as I wouldn't have got there in time, it would take a couple of hours or so to get there. I rang my mother as it is her mum and told her that nan is going and doesn't have long. She said that it will be a false alarm, but I pleaded with her to go before it's too late. She said she would ring the hospital later. I was stunned, I couldn't make her go or believe me! In hindsight I wonder if she didn't want to see her go. Within thirty minutes of my phone call to the hospital, my nan had passed away. I felt as though I couldn't cry anymore. I missed out on seeing her all these years and now we made it up and she has now gone. I always try and think that I saw her a couple of times before she passed away and that was a memory for me.

Next day I went to the hospital with my mum. My brother was there, and I had to keep myself calm as now was not the time. They pulled my nan out of the morgue drawer and then unceremoniously put her on a metal trolley with tissue over her body. Not a nice way to present her to us! We said our goodbyes to her and as I went to kiss her on the forehead, I noticed a tear from her eye. It had frozen on her face and her eyes were open and also glazed. I kissed her and said how cold she was and the tear on her face made me think she must have shed it as a release from this world. I must admit, it is a picture I see a lot in my head, when I think of her. There was no lovely setting, chapel of rest, but a frozen body on a metal trolley. We saw the mortician's take her out of the drawer. It was something that I would not wish on anyone.

We all went back to my grandad's house; bless him he was lost. My grandad gave me a photo album and showed me photos of my grandparents and me together. He wanted me to remember the good times we had. My brother was feeling put out with the attention I was getting. He was looking around the room as if he was 'casing the joint', looking for things he could have. I was aware of what he was doing and had to let him know I knew, in his ear. It was a heart-breaking day! I always say to people who are estranged, due to a family dispute etc, to try and make it up with each other as one day they will not be here, and you have lost them and the years of not seeing them.

Being stubborn isn't always the best way. I went back home, and the grief hit me. I listened to music and sang to get it out. One night I was talking out loud to my nan, saying I was missing her etc then all of a sudden, I looked to my right and there she was. Standing life like in my living room, she didn't speak but smiled and radiated peace and love. She was happy now and at peace. I said I was grateful to her for showing herself and visiting me. She then vanished and I was reeling that she came but knew she had to go and could not stay. A few days later it was my nan's funeral. It was hard as it always is, through the service my mother was stoic and did not show much emotion unlike my sister and me who struggled. I knew she was fine where she was. As soon as we came out of the crematorium, my mother just turned to me and fell on my shoulder and cried 'she's gone, she's gone'. I held her until she had finished crying, it was a release for her too. My mother did not have a close relationship with her mother. This was the end of the line for my mother and she knew at that moment what she had lost. It was pitiful as my mother is a strong woman.

We went to my grandad's house for the wake. My grandad after having a brandy, stood up in a full living room of relatives and said 'Karen, we brought you up, you lived with us, you are one of us', in front of his children and to my parents who didn't know where to look. I was choked, it had come full circle into the family. Everyone knew now that my grandparents brought me up for a few years on and off, this acknowledgement was a blessing to me but not my parents. I felt for them though as the relatives were looking at them. It was a sad day and I went into the front room to get away from everyone and feel my nan's energy, to reminisce of our time together in that room, playing together and chatting etc. My granddad unbeknownst to me followed me and put his arm around me and said, 'she loved you'. We both hugged each other, and he beckoned me into the other room to mix with the rest of the family.

A relative came up to me and confided in me that when they were in the kitchen, my brother was in there trying to sell videos of a nasty and violent nature to family members. I was mortified and so angry, I couldn't bring myself to go and see him as a presence was with me and said 'leave it and let it go', I knew it was my nan and I did as she said. To do that at our nan's funeral was disrespecting her memory. There are some things you cannot forgive or forget. I spent the rest of the day with my family and extended family, talking and bringing up memories of a long time ago. I said my goodbye's and then went back home to Wales.

I struggled a little with the thought of the lost years without my grandparents, but I knew you cannot change the past. As for my brother, I did not speak to him again! I did not see the spirit of my nan again either, but I was to find out that it was not the last time I would feel her presence.

I got on with my life and still went to Spirit Circle and to see a medium on a Saturday with Sara. I also sat in meditation circles at Sara's house. One day I went to Sara's house and her new boyfriend was sitting in her kitchen area. I said hello to him and after the usual chatting I got up to leave her house, I went to say goodbye to him and that is when I saw his aura. I was stunned to see anyone's aura but his aura was red, black and murky with a feeling that he had a lot of anger in him. I walked to the door and told Sara that I needed to talk to her outside. She came out and I told her what I saw and felt. She listened and said that she will be safe. A few days later, I went to see her, and she said that she had stopped seeing him as he was angry and possessive with her and it frightened her. Sometimes I still see auras on people and plants or living things.

I still had visitations in my house and when I was asleep or semi awake. My daughter Natalie was aware of spirit and energy being close to her. My friends would ask me if I could see anything for them etc and I would tell them if I do or if I see something in their absence, then I would tell them. Life plodded on as it does. Sara left Wales and moved to Newcastle for a new job. I carried on being aware of what I picked up on, messages and visions etc, but keeping it to myself or telling people who I trusted.

16. *You Are Not Alone*

One year later, Peter, Nat and I decided to go on holiday to Cyprus, but unbeknownst to Nat, who absolutely had a 'penchant' for anything Egyptian since she was a small child. I decided to surprise her with this trip as we booked two trips on a cruiser/ferry to Haifa/Jerusalem in Israel for me and Cairo for nat. Some months later we went to Cyprus, but when we got there the travel agent had told us that we could not go to Israel due to the recent troubles there, but we could still get to Cairo, to see the Pyramids of Giza, bazaars and the Cairo Museum. I thought great as Nat does not know, so it will be a very big treat for her.

On the day of the trip we set off early as we were being picked up and taken to Limassol where the cruiser was docked. As we got closer to the cruiser, Nat questioned where we were going. I said, 'it's a day out' and being vague. It was only when we got into the cabin on the cruiser that I told her where we were really going. She was shocked and very happy. I was pleased for her and didn't want to spoil her day by letting her know that I did not like boats, anything that puts you out to sea. I have been on mini ferries before and usually stand by the lifeboats with a drink in my hand, ready to jump in one. I wonder if I was on the Titanic in a previous life as I am really not good on them. To be on a journey such as this for eighteen hours was too long for me to think about, eighteen minutes is enough! As a parent you keep it in, and you get on with it.

We watched the cabaret on the night but all I could concentrate on was the sound of the engine of the boat. Peter and Nat slept well, but I had my eyes open not relaxing at all. I know it sounds mad, but I feel it strongly. Early the next morning, we docked at Port Said in Egypt. I got off as quick as I could and knelt down on the ground and kissed the cobbles of the port, just like the pope. The Egyptian port workers looked on bemused by this, I said my thanks to the heavenlies for keeping my family safe.

We all took to our coaches as there were quite a few of us holiday makers on this trip. We had to familiarise ourselves with our coach and driver. All three coaches were driven into the heart of Cairo, which took a couple of hours. The tour guide was then picked up from her local area. Cairo is manic, trucks with soldiers passing and guards standing on top of buildings, fast black and white taxis weaving in and out of the busy traffic, beeping loudly to whoever got in their way. We were told facts about Cairo from our tour guide and explained why buildings where people lived were standing with three walls and washing lines were precariously hanging from the outside wall that did not exist. What stops them falling out of the building whilst trying to grab their washing in the dark I do not know.

We went to a bazaar and bought some hieroglyphics on papyrus paper and some other mementos. We then went on to travel to the Pyramids of Giza. It is not like you see on the television or pictures; the surprising bit is they have built on the Sahara Desert. As you go over the River Nile on the bridge, you then see a few shops on a roundabout and then you go up a very long road to the pyramids and if you look to the right then that is when you see Pizza Hut at that angle. When photos are taken of the Sphinx and the Pyramids then you will know that they have their backs to the shops. We got off the coach and it was fifty degrees centigrade and it was midday, so a hat was needed. We walked to the pyramids and Nat was in awe of them and so were we. They are huge and the bricks that make them are large, yet you are not able to walk up them. Since this is not allowed understandably to preserve them, they have security police on camels that patrol the area.

An Egyptian man on his camel beckoned Nat to go and sit on his camel with him for a photo shoot for us to take, next to the pyramids. She sat on the camel and when I asked the man to take my daughter off the camel, he refused and asked for a lot of Egyptian shillings. We did not have this amount of money and I will not have my daughter be a bargaining tool either. I was telling him to give her back to me and we were having a heated debate, when all of a sudden, an Egyptian policeman in white uniform on his camel was bounding towards us, as he must have seen and heard what was going on. The man who had my daughter quickly let Nat off his camel and as he saw the policeman coming and to shut me up, he gave me a green wooden scarab beetle, one you would wear on a pendant and said 'take this for good luck' and he rode away before the policeman could get to him. I kept this scarab beetle in my shorts for the duration of the trip.

I went into a walk-in tomb and then went to see the sphinx which is so magical, and its face is now worn away due to the weather etc. We then as a group in our three coaches, went to the Cairo Museum. It is such a big place that you need a full day to see everything. Since it was packed with visitors, we only had a couple of hours or so to look around with our tour guide in tow. It was the case of looking at Tutankhamun's artefacts and his items, that were buried with him and to take photos quickly. It was interesting to see and hear, after a time the tour guide was calling the group and rounding us all up to go into our own groups as we had to leave to get on to the coach.

As we all made our way up the road to the coaches, we passed a street boy who was selling items. Everyone had passed him and not bought anything, and I felt sorry for him. I got to the coach and then said to my family "I will be back, wait for me". I ran back to the street boy and bought an alabaster sphinx, very heavy but thought Nat would love this in her bedroom. I paid the boy and thanked him and ran back to the waiting coach. The tour guide was not pleased with me. I then noticed that only one coach had stayed as the other two coaches had set off without us, my coach had gone. We started to travel again back to Cairo and that is when I realised that the three coaches were meant to stay together for safety and security reasons and now there was only our coach on its own.

We stopped in Cairo and the tour guide said, "I am going home now to make my husband's tea" and then left. I was stunned. We had a driver who spoke only Arabic and no English. I was sitting with my family in the back row of the coach and heard all of this. We all looked at each other and thought that this was not meant to happen.

Anyway, it was about 4pm and since it was late September/October it was still light but very soon it will be dusk. We travelled on for quite a while and then we started to travel in an area which was desert/scrubland. We were all chatting away to ourselves, then the coach stopped abruptly, and we did not know why. All of a sudden, the coach door opened and in came two men in some clothes that were not militia and they had AK-47 rifles in their hands. One stood in the doorway of the coach and aimed his rifle at the driver, shouting to him in Arabic and the driver shouted back at him but you could see that he was scared. He had no choice but to let them on. Since my family and I were sitting on the back row, I could not initially make out what the unfolding drama was about.

I then heard one of the men who looked as I would describe as a 'guerrilla' started shouting and being very threatening and started to point his rifle at the elderly couple seated at the front near the door. We did not know what he wanted. The elderly man shouted to him and said, 'we have nothing, we are old people, we have nothing'. The guerrilla then looked to the other side of the aisle and pointed his rifle to see yet again that they were elderly and of a pensioner age. The guerrilla slowly went down the aisle of the coach looking at people either side and pointing his rifle at them. This was unreal, that is when I realised that my daughter Nat and I were in trouble as we were the youngest, as I was in my thirties and Nat was nine years old. Peter, my husband was a lot older than me. I shoved Nat down on the floor right behind the seat in front of her and told her in no uncertain terms to stay down and keep quiet, no matter what she saw or heard.

I am in the exposed part of the back row and am sitting at the end of the aisle when all of a sudden, I look up and the guerrilla is at least two rows of seats away from me. He continues to walk down and looks at me and is aiming his rifle at me. I thought 'that's it, he has spotted me amongst the other holiday makers, he will not have my daughter whilst I am breathing'.

He stared at me which felt like forever and then he carried on looking at the people either side of me and then looked back at me as if he was looking through me, as if I was invisible. I held my breath realising he didn't see me, or did he? I didn't want him to hear me either. My eyes were fixed on his. He then turned his rifle away from us and then turned around and promptly walked away down the aisle to the door of the coach. He yelled at the driver and closed the door. Nat stayed where she was on the floor of the coach. I was frozen to the spot and couldn't believe what had happened and was invisible to him. The coach started to slowly move away and as it did, I gingerly moved my head sideways to look through the side window at the back, hoping they didn't see me this time. That is when it all hit me! What I saw I will never forget.

I saw quite a few guerrillas with AK-47s in a row, aiming them at a row of holiday makers made to stand against their coach. Some guerrillas were opening baggage at the boot of the coach and raiding these people's belongings, and the people looked understandably terrified. two coaches who went on ahead of us, who were meant to be in our group of three coaches. There were men smoking cigarettes nervously and women looking very scared. These were younger people not elderly like my group. One of the coaches was the one I was meant to be on. That could be why they didn't take our group off the coach as they realised our coach was made up of elderly holidaymakers. My god, it made sense now. I got upset to see the people standing against the side of their coaches, scared and not knowing what was about to happen to them. I felt helpless, but there was nothing I could do! Nat didn't see any of this thank god, as she stayed down. All of a sudden, the driver shouted something Arabic to us and turned our internal lights off on the coach. We were still in danger.

He put his foot down and accelerated to get out of the desert and out of danger. He then said in English, 'bandits, bandits', he was scared. He didn't say any more as it was getting dark now and he did not want our coach to be seen and attracting the 'bandits' with the lights on and turned off his headlights too and drove in the dusk. He was a very brave man. He sped up all the way to Port Said. No one on the coach spoke to each other due to fear, shock or both. Time was running out as we had to be at Port Said before the 6pm departure of the cruiser, we were in Egyptian waters and our visa expired at 6pm. If you stay in the country after this deadline then you will be arrested.

We arrived at the port and we all got off the coach and as I was near the end of the queue, I went to the driver and thanked him. I think he could see it on our faces and knew we thanked him in our way. We all ran as fast as we could to the jetty and got on the boat with a minute or two to spare. No sooner had we got on the boat, the ramp came up and that was it, we were off!

As soon as I turned around to see the port and the coach with the driver it all hit me. Had the guerrilla seen me and Nat, then what would have happened. The poor holidaymakers in the head-up coaches, what happened to them, how are they getting back, as their visas would have expired, who would find them? How did the guerrilla not see me and why did he look right through me as if I was invisible? Whilst I was taking this all in, I put my hand in my shorts pocket and took out the green scarab beetle. I held it and thought back what the man had said. 'Take this, it will bring you good luck'. I have had my thoughts about this, maybe he didn't see me like when I was a child and my mum didn't see me or when I was in danger.

Was it the scarab beetle or was I being watched over? I

believe somehow, we can appear invisible or wish to appear invisible, maybe our aura goes clear or comes so close to us that we are not detected.

I do not know the answer to this, but I did years later when I watched a film based on a book written by an American author, who actually made a character in the film who was in danger of being seen and either captured or killed. He was in full view of the South American guerrillas and they were literally feet away from him. He realised he was in danger and the game was up. Then in the film you see the guerrillas looking around him and did not see him, and for special effects they put in transparent layers around him as if he was invisible, his aura was invisible. The character was saying to himself 'they cannot see me'. The guerrillas walked off and left him to look elsewhere for him.

Why it happens, not always either, unless we must 'will' it, like positive thinking. I do not know the answers. Also, the other thought I had was why was our coach not part of the three coaches. I made our coach late originally due to me rushing back near the Cairo Museum to get the alabaster sphinx from the street boy. That is when the other two coaches decided to carry on without our coach and leave us behind, also the green scarab beetle with its bearer receiving good luck and of course the heavenlies watching over us, be it my nan or angels. I will always be grateful for their intervention. My family sat down together that night and did not talk about it, not to scare Nat and make her aware of what really went on and with the other two coaches left behind.

The next day I looked at the newspapers to see what happened to the others and there was no mention of the incident or them. Where are they? That is something I cannot find any details on. We carried on with our remaining days of our holiday, but I was disturbed by it all. We made friends as you do on holiday.

We went home and got on with our daily lives, but this was not the last time I stared death in the face.

LIVING IN TWO WORLDS

17. *Turning Point*

The following year we decided to go to the Mediterranean again, as we do love the Greek Islands. We decided to go to Corfu. It was July and in hindsight it was the wrong time of the year as it's so hot then. The Greeks stay in the shade, yet we do not as we love the sun. Nat goes in the pool or the sea like me. We were meeting people as usual, drinking, looking at Greek culture etc. Then one day as we were walking, we came across an area in a large cove area, where the beach was lovely and quite a few people were down there. We decided to stay here for a bit. We were standing on the cliff path which looks down onto the beach and cove, also a large rock formation in the shape of a tunnel. I said to Peter 'I want to swim in that tunnel/cave' but Nat said, 'No mum, I don't want you to go'. I then said, 'I won't be long'. I love adventures so I thought I would swim to the cave/tunnel and have a look around.

I got down the side of the cliff and walked onto the beach and swam all the way to the entrance of the tunnel. It is called Canal D 'Amour, tunnel of love.
I started to swim just inside the tunnel and saw how narrow the walls were getting as I went in further to see the exit of the tunnel which opens out into the sea. So, I started to swim towards it and all of a sudden, I got

sucked into an underwater whirlpool which was not visible above the water. I went down into the vortex of water and struggled to escape its clutches. In a short while it pushed me up to the surface as if to give me air, then it sucked me down again. My lungs were burning as they were filled with sea water. I knew I was drowning, as my lungs could not get any air now. My escape was nowhere near to be seen. I was losing my life as I was down in the vortex, thinking of my daughter and this will be the last time I see her. I then said in my head knowing I was drowning, 'please god, help me, I will work for you'. This thought took seconds to process as I felt myself fading. I then heard a man's voice in my head, loudly over the sound of the water vortex. He said, 'on the next time, (meaning when I pop up again to the surface for the last time), with all you might, throw yourself backwards'. This took seconds to register.

On the next pop up I gasped and did as I was instructed and threw myself backwards not knowing where I was in the cave. In sheer desperation, I did so, my arms were free and came up over my head. I grabbed the nearest thing I could feel and get to. It was the cave walls. I don't know where the strength came from as I was on the verge of passing out. I grabbed the walls of the cave with both hands again and pulled my body away from the vortex. I did it all again one more time. I must have made it to the entry to the cave as you cannot see inside the cave from outside. I heard muffled sounds of voices, then I passed out. The next thing I knew was that I was on the beach and two young men pumping my chest. They apparently saw me floating out of the cave, realised I was unconscious and put me on their Lilo and used it as a stretcher. They did CPR on me on the beach. I came around and brought up water that I had in my lungs. It took a while to realise where I was. The two lads were Italian, and they happened to be lying on their lilo's in the sea not knowing I was in the cave, until they saw me floating. When I did come around, I looked up at them and couldn't thank them enough. I hugged them and told them how grateful I was to them.

After a short while I got up and started to walk up the hill wearily to meet up with Peter and Nat, making out I was alright, as they could not see too much from the distance where they were. Yet Nat shouted at me saying 'I told you not to go in there'. She was right, she listened to her instincts, but I did not listen or adhere to mine. I hugged her and said that I was so sorry for what I did. I would not put myself or her in that position again. She said that she knew I was in danger whilst I was in there, she felt it strongly. I couldn't show her or tell her how bad it was etc and continued to hug her again and told her again and again that I love her. We all walked slowly back to our hotel and as I looked at the sea, lapping up the shoreline, I said to myself 'you have to respect the sea as she will take you'. We got back to the hotel, got showered and dressed up for the night's entertainment.

On the night I saw the holiday representative and told her about the Canal D Amour and its whirlpool and of course what had happened to me that day. She was mad with me in concern. She said, 'You should never go in there, it's dangerous'. There is a whirlpool in there where the two seas meet in the cave". Now it made sense why the whirlpool was there. She then said 'A young Italian boy went in there last week and he drowned'. I was horrified, the poor boy. It nearly took me, if it was not for the intervention of the voice who gave me instructions to get out of the whirlpool. I was shaken by this news. The Rep then addressed all the holiday makers in the room of the cabaret and instructed that no-one is to go in the Canal D' Amour cave as it is dangerous and relayed the story of the Italian boy's fate.

She didn't mention what had happened to me, but I got a side glance from her. Enough said I thought. It took me a few days to go back in the sea to swim because I had to make myself do it or if I didn't then I would not go into the sea ever again.

I got on with my life, being aware that I was being watched over and my life changed after that event. I worked full time as usual but knew there was more to this life than this. My friend Sue had told me about a night of Clairvoyance in a local pub and did I want to go with her as my birthday is in January so it would be a treat for me, I thought I am coming with bells on.

We were both in the queue to see the Clairvoyant and her daughter who was doing readings too. Sue turned around to me and said that she did not want a reading with the mother as she had heard some negative reviews, so she wanted a reading with the daughter instead. I was not fussed as I would be happy with a reading regardless who it was. Sue was called up and she went straight to the daughter and I then went to the mother. I sat down and was open to what I was about to hear. The lady started to tell me which I did not know much about in my family, then she dropped a bombshell of information that no else knew. She told me some personal things about Peter, and she proceeded to tell me that it will not change. She then said 'who is Steve', so I explained that my brother is called Stephen who does get called Steve. She said 'No, this someone else called Steve and he is a Jack the Lad, not a bad lad but he is going to come into your life if he hasn't already'. I was nonplussed, I thought why would he come into my life?

As she was nearing the end of the reading, she dropped another bombshell. She also said, 'You will leave your husband by Christmas'. I nearly choked on my drink of pop. Leaving Peter, I knew things were not going smoothly recently but this I did not foresee. She was adamant on this remark. I thanked her, picked up her leaflet with her mobile number on and met up with Sue at the other end of the pub. Her face said it all. She said that she was not happy with her reading at all. She said it did not relate to her. I had to tell her that mine was very good and that she told me that I would leave Peter, and someone called Steve would come into my life. She was shocked but not as much as me. We both had a few more drinks especially after my shock reading and then we both went home.

A couple of weeks later I started to go on the internet and talk to people on chat rooms as it was a social thing in those days. You made friends in a way, from across the globe too. I was having problems with my P.C and I was clueless when it came to trying to sort it out and thought if I ask someone in the chatroom then they may be able to talk me through it. I put out a request for help of any sort to remedy the problem. Whilst I was hoping someone types back to me with a solution, I carried on chatting to people.

I was about to sign out as I needed to do my tea when a person replied to me and said they can talk me through how to sort out my P.C. I thought brilliant, I can get it sorted. It was a man and he was friendly, and he said he was about to leave the same chatroom and then he saw my request. We started talking about my query and we sorted it out. Then we both started talking about our families and our lives, where do we live etc. There was nothing in it, just being friendly and we agreed to chat again the next time we came to the chat rooms. He had a good sense of humour and he thought I was funny too. We just clicked. We did not know each other's real names, so we called each other by our nicknames in the chatroom. Some days I did not go on and sometimes Peter went on his chat rooms. The thing is with Peter, I was aware that he was seeing a woman who he worked with, but I did not let on I knew, maybe I was hoping it would fade away. He used to say to me 'I should not have married you as I wanted a woman with money', I thought he was joking but the look on his face said differently. It seems that this woman he was seeing had money, if it was love I do not know.

I carried on living my life with Peter and also talking to my new friend, when I decided to ask him what his name was, and he was called Steve. I thought nothing of it as we were just friends. There was no intention from either side to get close, but it happened. We felt that we had been together before in a previous life, it does happen.

Many months later, just after Christmas, Peter and I had split up and Steve and I were a couple. It was hard for Natalie, I did feel bad about the situation, but I hoped she would understand. It was the beginning for me to do more spirit work.

Steve was travelling down to see us every weekend when possible, and on one   particular evening I was not feeling well. I rang Steve and told him what was going on with me. He must have put his foot down in the car to get to me within two hours. I told him I believed my heart was being erratic and so I rang for an ambulance as I could not get to the main hospital in Shrewsbury as it is thirty miles away. Steve and Nat were following the ambulance in Steve's car.

I was being attended to in the ambulance and we had been in transit for a while when I knew I was leaving my body. I knew I was dying. I told the paramedic who stood over me, that I was dying. I had gone through this when I was fourteen years old, so you know when you are going. I couldn't breathe. He did not believe me, I told him again that I knew I was going. All of a sudden, I heard the noise that is associated with you leaving the body and I felt like I was sinking into the ambulance trolley. Too late I was leaving without him believing me.

I was on the E.C.G at the time when it made an alarm noise and he jumped up and saw that I had flat lined. My heart had stopped which brought me back to his attention. I then rose above my body and was on top of the inside of the ambulance watching on. I saw the paramedic shout to the driver, and he stopped the ambulance. I then saw the paddles to shock me back, being attached to my chest and they tried a couple of times. I heard the whooshing sound again and the pull downwards and I was apparently back in my body, but I was not conscious. I do not remember much after that, and certainly not the journey to the hospital. I started to come around just before I got to the hospital and I looked at the paramedic who I spoke to before I went. I was exhausted but I did look at him and said, "I told you I was going". He just looked bewildered and looked at me in a way of how I knew and thank god you are back.

When I was in the hospital being checked over and the paramedics were giving their 'handing over' information to the doctors, Steve had said to me that the ambulance had stopped, and he knew I was in trouble. I told him that I knew as I left my body and watched on. I comforted Nat and said I was fine. As for Steve, what a start to our relationship, yet it made us stronger and we knew we wanted to be together even after this.

LIVING IN TWO WORLDS

18. *I'm Here*

Nat and I were going back to a city environment which I did not take to straight away, after being in a small village in the countryside. For Nat this was the right move for her to grow into the young woman she is today. Also, I had two stepchildren, Beth and Sam who used to come over on Saturdays which gave Steve a chance to see them.

I had only lived here for a few months and was living in a rented place when a situation in the family arose which was quite upsetting. It was the day before the meeting, not knowing how it will go. I was in the bedroom sorting out some clothes, when all of a sudden, I was aware that someone was watching me from the doorway. I looked up to see a large framed man, with a slight hump in his back and very big eyes. He looked at me and he said something I could not understand due to his accent being a very strong Yorkshire accent. I heard this in my ears and not in my head. It sounded like 'it be reet and he had said it twice, and with that comment he slowly disappeared into thin air! I was thinking who are you and what did you just say?

I carried on tidying for a bit, with the picture of the man

in my head. My partner Steve came in from shopping and bought some cigarettes, so we both went outside. Steve came out to see me on the doorstep as I must have looked preoccupied. I told him I had a visit from spirit, he didn't believe in the spirit world nor the afterlife, so he was not going take me seriously, so I thought 'leave it'. We both went into the kitchen after and as he was buttering his bread for a sandwich, I decided to tell him in some detail. I explained how the man looked and was hunched over and with his big eyes, and I told him what I had interpreted from what he had said. He dropped the knife and went as white as the bread he was buttering. He got a bit anxious and said what did he say? I said I couldn't understand what he had said for his strong accent. I repeated what he had said and the way he said it in my best Yorkshire accent. Steve said, 'that's my granddad', I said what did he say or mean by it, and Steve broke it down for me and said it was 'it will be alright', just that the words were cut out and the sentence shortened. I asked for a photo of his granddad as he appeared in solid form to me. I once again described him in full detail and then a photo was given to me. I said, 'That's the man I saw'. Steve was shocked and a little upset as he was very close to his granddad who had died some years earlier. He went quiet for a while and was thinking over what I had said.

It was a long and worrying night as the next day was to

be a stressful day. The next day came and we both attended the meeting and the outcome was positive. It was only when I got home, I said, 'he was right, your granddad he said it will be alright'. We both agreed. It wasn't to be the last time spirit intervened or helped us. Nat and I saw spirit and I explained to Nat that it was normal to see them, but Steve did not.

One day whilst I was at work, Nat was putting washing out on the line, and as she got up from picking up an item of washing, she was eye level to a window. She jumped with shock as in front of her in the window stood a lady who smiled at her, she was in my bedroom. Nat ran into the house and wouldn't go back outside until I got back home from work and left the washing where it was. Nat was about twelve years old then and I can understand that it had frightened her. I got home and calmed her down. I said that the lady would not harm you. She described her to me, and I made a mental note of this.

A few months later, I was outside putting the washing on the line and sure enough, the lady was once again in my bedroom standing further away from the window but stood there in solid form and looked at me. I thought it was her and I knew she stood back from the window this time as it still shocks you when they are that close to you and you are not expecting it. I said hello to her and then she smiled and disappeared. I felt her presence a lot after this but did not see her. There was one visitor who kept me on my toes.

I was sitting alone in my living room and started thinking about the baby boy I had lost, my son. No sooner had I thought it, I looked across the room and there stood a young man with white blonde hair and black eyes wearing a long black coat. This frightened me as I was not familiar with black eyed spirit. He didn't speak to me but looked straight at me. I said, 'I don't know who you are, but you are not of this earth and I want you to go'. He left and this incident has never left my mind. If it was my son, why were his eyes black? I didn't tell anyone as I felt best not to worry them.

One day I went to see my family and my grandad as he was living on his own now. He used to tell me about the house that my nan and grandad lived in years ago and how my nan used to talk to the spirit visitors and residents there, just like I do. My mum does not want to converse with spirit and does not want to know about them. It seems natural to me like breathing. I loved talking to my grandad, I thought the world of him, especially after the lost years. He was living in sheltered housing and he wouldn't mix with the 'oldies" as he would call them, in the dining room as he liked his own company. He went out most days and was a fearless man, he was young at heart which is where I get it from. He was in his mid to late eighties.

I visited him one day and he let slip that a man had pointed a gun to his face in the street and demanded money from him. My grandad stood his ground and told him that he had no money but cigarettes. The man was having none of it and again demanded money by threatening my grandad. Once he realised that my grandad was not going to hand over his money or he did not have any, the man decided to pistol whip him around the head. I was mortified to see the marks on his face and head. I was so angry at this, I said, 'tell me what he looks like'' and I was about to rush out to find this violent thug, even though I would not have found him. My grandad said, 'leave it Kaz it's done'. I didn't agree but I said, 'Karma will come and what goes around comes around'. I don't wish harm on anyone but what you put out, you get back, good and bad.

Some months later, we had a visit from a couple who said they were selling our rented property and the property was originally her mother's until she died a couple of years previously leaving it for the daughter to rent it out. They had now decided to move to Derbyshire. I explained to the lady about the elderly lady I had seen and described her to her and she acknowledged that it was her mother and she was shocked to say the least. I told her she visited the place as she had happy times here and she confirmed that she did not want to leave the place but had to go into a home. We left it at that.

Steve and I were getting close to our deadline for leaving the property and we could not afford the bond that a lot of landlords were asking for near Nat's school. Then one day Steve had a meeting with his ex-wife and she happened to say that she wanted to move from her house and did we want to take it off her hands, pay her share of it as the other half of the share was Steve's already, as he left it to her previously and then she could move to another house. He agreed and came home to tell me what had transpired. I was a bit apprehensive but then thought of the timing of this decision as he had not mentioned that we needed to find a place. Spirit moves in mysterious ways. So sure, enough we finalised the transaction through a solicitor and legally bought the house on the day we were meant to leave our rental property. We were watched over that day too. As I said they can help in times of strife. We were handed the keys that day and unloaded the van.

We were in the kitchen and Nat was upstairs. I hugged Steve and was relieved that we had somewhere to live and it was a very long day. I looked over Steve's shoulder and in the doorway of the kitchen behind Steve, stood a very tall man, standing still, staring at me in his trilby hat, long coat and he was in a black silhouette form. I thought we had visitors, I told Steve and he was not impressed. The man then disappeared so we kept it to ourselves. It took us a while to settle into our house. It didn't take long for our previous residents to make themselves known. This house was built in 1920 so has had a lot of residents. One night I was leaving the living room to go into the hall, and when I looked to the right I saw a young man walking up the stairs, he was wearing a brown suit and he said 'I'm off to bed now' I heard this in my ears. I thought ok, and I bent my neck to watch him go all the way up the stairs to the landing. I stood in the hallway laughing to myself, thinking who was that, bless him! I didn't tell anyone as I thought they are probably tired of me telling them things.

A few months later Nat and I were in the living room, watching the television whereupon a man in his 40's, wearing a shirt and a knitted tank top and pleated trousers, walked past us, he then walked across the other side of the room and walked into the opposite wall, then in through to next door's house. Nat looked at me and I looked at her and we just sat there, not sure what to say. We knew we had a busy house and future years showed us that too.

LIVING IN TWO WORLDS

LIVING IN TWO WORLDS

19. *Testing Times*

I started work in a new job and didn't tell anyone that I spoke to spirits and picked up energy until one day, I had a premonition of a lady going into labour and I felt it was for one of the men in the office upstairs, who I did not know well. He would think I was mad, so I left it for a while. I was walking up the corridor on my floor and I saw the man I needed to tell. I asked him how he was, and he said he was fine, but his wife was pregnant, and she was due to give birth in a few weeks' time. In that second, I was shown in my third eye the premonition again, but this came with more detail. The baby's cord was around its neck, but the nurses could not see it and she was pushing. I grabbed his arm and said " please don't think I'm mad or to worry you but I dreamt about your wife who I do not know and you must know that the cord will be around the baby's neck, you must look out for this". He looked at me, stood back and thought where that had come from. He didn't say anything and walked off. I went home and felt I did the right thing.

I then attended a course at college and learnt Reiki when one day a student tried to give it to me and she told the tutor that something was pushing her away. I knew I had Spiritual Healing around me, and I used it as it is different to Reiki.

Weeks later I was at work and the man upstairs came down to see me and he was a bit het up. I thought I had upset him. He called me into an empty meeting room to speak to me in private. He sat down and excitedly told me that his wife had given birth to a girl and sure enough the cord was around her neck and she was in distress. The nurses couldn't see this just like my premonition. He was so excited to tell me. He said, 'The baby is fine but how did you know it was going to happen.!'. I told him what I am about, and he took it in. I told him not to tell anyone and he said he would keep it to himself. I see things for others but not for myself. This I was about to find out.

The previous day at work was long as I had a really bad headache which would not go away. The next day I thought I would have off sick and rest my head in the hope it went away. It did calm down and I went to my next-door neighbour to have a cup of tea. After our usual chat I got up and went to put the cup in her kitchen sink, when all of a sudden, I went a little strange. I couldn't put the cup straight down, and my face went numb and I went weak. She was alarmed at this and sat me down. She kept an eye on me and after a short while I said 'I'm going home'. So, I started to go home as I knew I wasn't right. I had not long got in and all of a sudden, my head felt like it was imploding and I could not get myself together anymore. My legs had gone, and I knew I was in trouble.

I rang 999 for an ambulance and it came quite quickly I think as I really have not got much recall after this. I had a CAT brain scan and they were thinking it was a SubArachnoid Haemorrhage, a bleed on the brain. I lay on the bed in the ward and I did not know what to think etc. I asked them to ring Steve but tell him I am ok. He turned up at the hospital with Nat. Then I had to have seven Lumbar punctures in my spine as the junior doctor kept on putting the needle in the wrong places in my spine. It did hurt and on the sixth time he did it, he hit a nerve in my back which made my left leg shoot out. Then a Neurology doctor saw what was going on and shouted at the doctor as he was doing it in the dim light from the window and not had a bed light on to see what he was doing. I said to the Neurology doctor on this seventh time that this will be the last one as I cannot do this anymore. He reassured me that this will be the last time. He put the long needle up my spine for the last time and withdrew the fluid out to be sent to the lab.

I was in a bad way then and had to lie down for hours. A Neurology doctor came to see me and told me that I had a Brain Haemorrhage that was on the outside of my brain and they think the bleeding has stopped and they had told

Steve that he had to go home as I had to rest. They came to see me during the night and kept an eye on me. A doctor woke me up in the night and confirmed that there was bleeding outside of the brain and he felt it had stopped. I must have slept afterwards.

A day or so later I was trying to get up to go to the loo and help a lady who could not reach her water jug as the nurses were so busy elsewhere. I did this and when I got back to my bed, I started to feel strange again. I got into bed and then my right side of my body was numb, my brain was not functioning properly, I couldn't think straight, couldn't get my words out and couldn't move my right arm and leg. I lay my head on the pillow and tried to get the attention of the lady next to me. This took a long while and then she looked at me and realised I couldn't talk to her. I must have made a noise and she rang the buzzer for the nurses. They came over and I tried to tell them what I felt and all of a sudden, a nurse called for a doctor. He came over and after checking me over, calmly said 'you have had a stroke'.

It was like a bolt out of the blue. What the hell is happening.

I was taken to the CAT brain scan again and they said you have had one, which could have been caused by the haemorrhage. I was put in a Neurology ward and they kept an eye on me. I was in there for a week or so until they put me in a room on my own for peace and quiet.

Once I was up out of the bed, they took me to a room to show me how to put a kettle on and how to do simple household jobs so I can then tackle these at home. Once I was discharged, I was in my bed for a few months , Steve tells me. He did not have any help, nor did he know what to do to rehabilitate me.

One day I had to return to the Neurology Department to see the doctor, whilst waiting there a nurse came to me to see me and quietly said 'I am so sorry about what happened to you on that ward, it should not have happened'. It was negligence basically. She was so upset and explained that she was there when I had my botched lumbar punctures and then my stroke. I tried to tell her that it was not her fault but the doctor who did it. She knew I was upset too. She then walked away quickly not to be seen. The Neurology doctor saw me in his room and said it will take time to get better and he showed me a leaflet about a brain injuries unit called Second Chance. I took this home with me and thought about it as I could not say the right words and could not cope with noise and fast movement. I could not feel with my right side still.

I was taken to the Second Chance unit and I saw some poor souls who have had massive strokes and other brain injuries that I felt they had for such a long time. I looked at one lad and he could not do anything for himself. That was it for me. I went to the unit once again and it made me think to myself that I have got to fight to get better.

I went home and I cried and then I thought that's it now no more tears. I then remembered a film I watched years earlier called the 'Patricia Neal Story' where her husband Roald Dahl rehabilitated her after she had 3 strokes that made her unable to speak etc. He was hard on her by re teaching her the basics of things like talking, working out and saying the right words, walking, picking things up etc. It was like someone had put this in my head. That was the moment I said to myself you will make yourself walk, talk, get the right words to come out of my mouth etc.

My workplace was good to me as they kept my job open for me, for my return if and when I was ready to come back. Every time I got a word wrong I would say it over and over again until I got it right and Steve helped me with my words, I hung on to things as I tried to get myself to walk, I still could not feel heat on my right side, so one day when a bath was being run for me, I put my hand in the water and the bath water was scolding hot yet I could not feel it. I pulled my arm out of the bath and my hand was red and scolded. It blistered badly for days afterwards and the skin was not the same for a long time. I learnt quickly after that, it was not a playground in my house, there was danger in the kitchen and bathroom with hot water etc. Nat was at school and when she did come home, she went out to see her friends. I think it was her way of dealing with what was going on at home.

Steve went back to work, which again must have been a reprieve for him from dealing with my problem. One day I felt that I had to try and walk as far as I could, I opened the front door for the first time in months and shuffled my way to the lamp post in the street. I grabbed the lamppost and fell against it. I shed a tear or two in relief that I had reached it. I did it again, and this was the start of my walking. After a few months of all the pushing myself to do things, Steve took me out and we went to a shop in a big shopping mall. He went to get something from another shop, and I was standing at the till to pay for my item and everyone was huffing and puffing as I could not remember what to do. I opened my purse and the coins were there, but I could not work out what coins I had to give the cashier. It was like being a child again and I got frustrated as I really struggled so I gave the shop girl my purse and asked her to get the coins that I needed to hand over. She did so but the people behind me were tutting and huffing as I was taking too long. Had I been my usual self before the stroke I would not have been bothered but this really upset and angered me. I was humiliated as I could not do something simple like that. Steve met me out of the shop, and I said, 'don't leave me again, I cannot do that again'. We both agreed that I won't be alone again until I was on the road to recovery hopefully. I am so aware of queues now that if someone might be struggling due to health conditions etc, to be patient.

I gradually learned new things, as they say if a part of your brain dies then it tries to compensate for another part of your brain. I noticed that my taste in food had changed, I could do something's I couldn't do before, my handwriting is different and its really strange but I have a capacity to remember things down to the smallest detail and even things which if I went to a music quiz I could tell them some things which are banal. Anyway, Kaz was back but different in some ways.

I eventually went back to work and lasted there for about an hour or so then a good friend used to see me struggle and say, 'come on now Kaz, time to go home'. No argument from me there and then she took me home. They were very patient with me at work. I gradually started to last out at work a few hours a day and worked myself to be at work for a full day. I still went blank on some things, but I eventually slowly got back to my duties. The girls in the office were good to me even though I think they did not know what to expect. I got on with life and I did gradually improve.

20. *Business As Usual*

The next year I started to see my family again and Grandad. It was good to see them. I made a few visits to my Grandad's flat and we talked about old times and new times too. I was getting more confident in travelling on public transport and getting about in Birmingham even though it is a fast pace of the city.

It was May Day Bank Holiday and I got up early as Steve and I were planning to go out for the day in the car. I was soaking in the bath, when all of a sudden, I saw my Grandad in the bathroom in front of me and he was lying down struggling to breathe. I heard him say 'Help me, help me'. I shot bolt upright in the bath and was upset and shocked. I got washed, dressed and ran downstairs, I told Steve what happened, and I started to ring my Grandad's phone number but there was no answer. I didn't know the number for the home. My heart was racing, and I was thinking is this a future event or is it like my Nan, real time happening. I tried a lot of times to get hold of him and I found the number for the sheltered housing and rang that but no answer. Steve asked me what I wanted to do, so I thought about it and said that if we go out for a few hours, then I will make phone calls periodically on my mobile phone.

So, we went out and was in the middle of nowhere in North Yorkshire. When all of a sudden, I felt this heavy weight on me, and I knew what it was. I turned to Steve as he was driving the car and I calmly said, 'My Grandad has died'. He looked at me shocked and stopped the car. I then said it again and I knew I was right. I can't describe the feeling or knowing but it weighs on you. He said, 'what do you want to do', I said 'There is nothing I can do, he has gone'. We sat in the car for a minute and then I walked out of the car and walked on my own up a country lane and cried and said 'I love you Grandad, you are going to be with Nan, I am sorry I was not there with you'. I got back in the car and noted the time of when I knew he had died.

We went back home, and I was not myself. I went to the house phone and saw we had a message on the answering machine. I listened to it and it was my Mum. She proceeded to tell me that my Grandad (her dad) had passed away this morning at about 11'o'clock. This was the time I told Steve in the car, and I was so upset as I knew he had. He came to see me in the morning before he died. My Mum had then said that he was in hospital with a chest complaint and had trouble breathing. That is what I saw as I was in the bath. I told her and I said he was asking for help and I could not help him from where I was. She said I would not have made it in time to the hospital due to the distance where we live. I was devastated, I felt like why I could not get through to the home not knowing he was in the hospital, I wish I could have helped him somehow. We all go through these thought processes when we lose someone, yet when we have time to think later it is only then we realise that we could not do anything.

I then started to sit in a spirit circle and started to get messages for people in the circle and learn what I thought I had lost, but it was still there in my head. I did stand up Mediumship, which means standing in front of a room full of people who are awaiting a message from their loved ones in spirit and passing messages on to them.

I do prefer one to one reading where I feel that you can say personal information that they can relate to as evidence of life after death and comfort them. I found I heard and saw spirit more after my Brain Haemorrhage.

One particular reading I did, was for a good friend's sister whose husband had died a couple of years previously. As I started with psychometry and held her late husband's watch, whilst talking to her, I noticed that I felt physical changes to my body. I started to feel broad in my chest and my face was changing. My voice also changed into a man's tone. I then leaned over the table and held her hand and said personal things to her. I was aware I was doing this, but it felt right, and I felt an overwhelming emotion for this woman, it wasn't something I would normally have done. I knew it was not just me in my body, sitting opposite this lady. The lady called me by her husband's name and held on to my hand too for an instance. I knew her husband was talking through me. This went on for a short while and I had to come back fully to my body.

Once I composed myself, I saw the lady was upset and happy at the same time. She was shocked at what had happened and so was I too. She said that my face had changed to his face, I had his voice as he was using my voice box in a trance state. He also grabbed her hand through me and said things to her that needed to be said. She said her husband was alive for that while. I apologised for the reading turning out the way it did and not knowing I would go into a semi trance state. She was absolutely delighted that it happened. This was a learning curve for me. The lady still tells people what happened that day years later.

It prompted me to attend a Trance Mediumship course to see how to do it correctly and safely. This was an eye opener, I had to sit in a cabinet in a red lit room full of people watching on. I then had to ask my guide to protect me and then partly allow my spirit to stand aside and allow for the waiting spirit to come in to use my body for communication. There was absolute silence in the room until I started to relax, and my face started to change. The people in the room were saying things amongst themselves and I could hear them saying she is now a man, and then a woman of different cultures. They also said they could see spirits behind me ready to take their turn. It was an extraordinary experience, I felt their personality, thoughts and what they wanted to say. It is hard to relax knowing that someone is going to borrow your body for a while. I learnt a lot that day and maybe so did the other recipient's in spirit. I have done Trance Mediumship a few times since and sometimes Spirit gets a bit impatient and wants to make me talk in a different accent whilst I am doing a reading.

There was one night where I really did not know what to do! I was in bed and got up for my usual visit to the toilet which was about 3am, (spirit is prevalent about in the early hours between 2-4 am). As I came back to the bedroom door I saw standing in the corner of the room, looking at Steve in the bed asleep, was a very tall monk who was disfigured and then had very large eyes and he was wearing a hooded gown. He then realised I was standing at the doorway staring at him and he turned his head and then stared at me. I did not like the feel of him at all. I said in my head 'you have three seconds to get out of my house, I will look away and by the time I look back you will be gone'. I looked back and sure enough he was gone. My heart was banging, I then checked to see if Steve was okay, luckily, he was still fast asleep. I thought, how would I explain this to him. I did not see the monk again that night until a few nights later, I woke up to see him on Steve's side of the bed and peering over him as he slept. I said in my head 'leave him alone', he then glided around the bed towards my side and then left through the bedroom door. That was when I thought he needed to be sent over.

A few days later I saw two mediums who I knew very well to do a ritual to move the monk over to the spirit world. The mediums did their crossing over service and when they were leaving my house, I asked them about him, and they did not want to talk about him, and I got the impression that it was not a pleasant experience and not to give him credence. I did not think about him either for that purpose. I then studied books and books about Soul Rescue and crossing spirit over to the spirit world. I learnt from these and spoke to others who did this also. I did not realise that this was something I was going to do in the future.

I continued to work full time, sit spirit circle, give readings, mediumship, clairvoyance and family life with all its dramas. I started giving healing and studying reflexology at college once a week for a year and then qualified. I did voluntary work at the Well Woman clinic to help ladies cope with pain and holistically treat them. I thoroughly enjoyed this work.

One time I was giving healing to a lady on the massage couch when all of a sudden I saw an elderly lady in full spirit form standing on the other side of the couch and she put her hands on mine, she then looked at the lady patient and then looked at me, smiled at me and said 'thank you'. She knew the lady patient and was happy that I was healing her. I would sometimes see any physical blockages, illness etc if I touched an area of the patient's body, yet I could not diagnose the problem with the patient as I am not a doctor. I would sometimes ask them after the healing if they had any query in that area and they would say yes. I would then ask them in a neutral way to look into it by checking it out with a doctor. I had my regular ladies who would return for healing.

One night though a lady who I had seen weeks before came to see me and said that she had seen the doctor after my advice and for what I had seen in her. She then told me that there was a health problem and luckily it has now been found and in the process of medical intervention. She hugged me and said thank you as she was going to leave it and not get it checked out until I asked her to. I was so pleased for her and I thanked spirit for their help and intervention. I found that my spirit work was taking a path I needed to go down.

Spirit was with me when I was on holiday too. Steve and I were in Cyprus, staying in an apartment that we had rented from Steve's friend. His friend had said that when we were over there, to check on a lady he knows, who lives alone over there. We said we would and we met up with Brenda, such a lovely lady she was. We were out drinking in a bar one dinnertime with her and I felt that I needed to tell her that I had her husband with me, who wanted to give her a message. Easier said than done when broaching the subject with someone you do not know well or if they are a believer. So I casually told her what I do apart from my full time job, and she was willing for me to give her a reading at her apartment. On the day that I was to see her, I asked Steve to stay in a bar and I will see him later. With spirit, when they come through, I could be giving information for an hour or so, as their timeline is different to ours. I get lost on time as the information is more important than keeping an eye on the clock. If spirit wants to say something, then I say tell me, it's your time to speak. That one window for them to appear for someone is precious for both persons.

I held her late husband's watch and chain and away it went. He came through singing a song, 'Im Henry the eighth I am'. I started to sing it to her in a cockney accent, not very tuneful I must admit. She sank back into her chair with her mouth open. She said 'That is the song he used to sing all the time'. I was pleased with the evidence that I gave to her. He gave me his personality and she could relate to it as he was a playful person. He then relayed to me how he died. He had a heart attack, which he thought was indigestion so he carried on his business of the day. Then the pain was quick and crushing and before he knew it, he had collapsed and died on the spot. He told me that he did not suffer and he is well now and he is his usual self. Brenda was so relieved at this fact as she did not want to think he suffered as she believed he did. I continued to give the information he gave me to give to her and she also felt his presence in the room too. It was his chance to get close to her and relay his love to her while he could. It was a lovely moment to see. I will never take for granted the gifts I have been given and to see the faces of the people whose loved ones paid a visit to see them with comforting words, this is something I will never forget.

Another time, I was in Gran Canaria, when I was at a time share conference, just checking out a resort with some reps. We were talking over a drink and all of a sudden I said to the lady rep, 'Give me your keys as I have a message for you'. She gave me her keys as I use Psychometry and the vision came through. I then said 'You have been to Florida recently and I saw alligators and a lot of house keys, you are walking into these houses'. She looked at me shocked and said 'Yes we have both been to Florida recently and we are looking into doing real estate over there for a living'. Her partner was the man sitting next to her at our table. He was open mouthed and nodded his head in agreement.

I explained that it was a future event and to watch out for it. She then said thank you and we left it at that. Steve was looking at me during the reading and smiled. He is accepting of my gift but I do not always approach people unless I feel that they need to know something if spirit thinks it is urgent, and they need to be aware of events to happen. Sometimes I see illness in people and I send them absent healing to them. Saying that, I do know that free will is paramount and sometimes as hard as it sounds, their life path is not my business to change.

I did one reading years ago where the family did not know what had happened to their sister as she was in a different country when she died. The sister came through to me and showed me literally how she died. I was very upset with what she had shown me, it was so horrific that I could not imagine what she went through. I had to contain my emotions very quickly, and as a human being, to not show any upsetting emotion on your face is very hard to do but it is necessary. I thought how on earth am I going to tell the siblings what had happened to their sibling with all the gory details. I was told by spirit to speak my truth, they need to know. I took a deep breath and then proceeded to concentrate on the one sibling who was the strongest. I explained that she was found with her head nearly decapitated. She was not found for a while. She took it on board and I had to tell her about how it happened. To my surprise, the sibling accepted the information and said 'I was told about that bit by the police over there'. I felt so sorry for her as she knew this and the thought of it was upsetting. I saw everything and I must admit this did upset me greatly but not until I left their house did I relive it. It is a picture in your head that you have to get used to. People dying in violent circumstances is very hard to release from your memory.

LIVING IN TWO WORLDS

21. *Previous Lives*

I was noticing that I was seeing glimpses of what I felt was a previous life. I felt I did not belong to my family when I was a child, but this was different. I started to see images being 'holed up' in a hall for the night, with an open roaring fire, drinking and raising our tankards and saying, 'To the King'. The men were wearing cavalier hats, and 3/4 trousers to the knee, knee length boots, big feathers in their hat and a long tunic uniform. They were getting prepared for their battle the next day to whom I did not know. I saw this on and off for a couple of years.

Then one day Steve and I went out for a drive around East Yorkshire, to areas I did not know, when all of a sudden, I started to feel sick and uneasy with emotion. I knew it was not me and I felt it was the area. I then shouted, 'stop the car', which he did, and I ran across the road, as I felt drawn to a spot, wherein in front of me was a field and I knew that I had been here before. The emotion was strong, and in front of me in my mind's eye I saw a battle where men were fighting and dying too. There were Cavaliers on horses, on foot and they were fighting men in a different uniform, dome shaped metal helmets and held very long poles with a spike on them. By now Steve had caught up with me, I told what I could see and feel with the field and that it felt familiar to me in a long-distanced memory. He took it all in and said this area was fought in the English Civil War. I did not know anything about the Civil War, it was not mentioned in history classes in my senior school, nor did I know of it in my learning as an adult.

We walked to the left and sure enough there was a sign explaining the historical event in the field from the 1600s. There was a battle between the Royalists who fought for King Charles the 1st and the opponent was the Parliamentarians who fought for a man called Oliver Cromwell. He was anti royals as he felt King Charles was flamboyant in his ways, yet Oliver Cromwell was puritan in his ways. The sign explained that many died in the field, and it was the battle of Marston Moor. I felt I was there in the thick of it. This was not to be the last time I felt my past life as a Cavalier.

Whilst I sat in the Spirit circle in the evening, the group did scry in a mirror. Everyone took their turn and we all stood on the side, looking at the person's reflection in the mirror. We had asked for protection as we did this and asked our previous life form to appear. I saw people's faces changing as the spirit form stood in front of their face, this is called Transfiguration.

I saw my face as a man who wore a cavalier brimmed hat and feather and uniform. Thing is, so did everyone else.

It was not my imagination. I thought you are never far away from me. I also sat for trance and in one group they saw my face and again I changed into a cavalier again.

I have seen past life recalls for Steve too by accident though. He was lying down on the settee with his head on a pillow on my lap, when I put my hands under the back of his head. No sooner had I done this; I saw a movie like a memory of one of his past lives. As it was happening, I relayed the information to him. He was in a situation of danger; he was wearing a grubby billowy shirt and kilt standing on the verge of a lake. It was dusk and he was standing near the banks of a castle which sat high up on the hill. He was a lookout, then all of a sudden, he spotted someone and said out loud, 'Montrose is coming, Montrose is coming'. He ran with all his might up the steep hill to get back to the castle and let the men protecting the castle to get ready for battle from this 'Montrose' and his men. I got the names Dun something. Dunvegan? I tried to get the full name, but it was not clear. It did sound like Dunvegan. I had never heard of this place. I have also had another vision when he is a sailor on a large ship and in battle with cannons going off.

A few months later, Steve and I went to Inverness in Scotland for a well-earned break and one day we decided to drive over the bridge to the Isle of Skye for the day.

We drove around the island taking the scenery in and stopping at places for photos etc.

It was in the afternoon and we had been driving aimlessly, when all of a sudden, I said that I had to get out of the car. Steve stopped the car and I dived out of my seat and ran straight ahead of me, the urge to run was so strong as I do not run normally, not a pretty sight. I felt my legs were not mine, I had to run to get to a place in the distance. I reached a place where there was a river and countryside and then I saw the sign far away, the sign said Dunvegan Castle. I was so shocked, this was Dunvegan Castle, the castle I had seen and heard the name of in Steve's past life recall. Steve had caught up with me by then and he was wondering what was up with me. I then pointed to the sign and he then remembered what I had said months previously. We both stood there in disbelief. The sign and castle could not be seen from where we were in the car as it was away from the road and bushes etc masked the panoramic view. I told him; this is where you were once before many years ago. He took it all in, thank god that he believes me even though he has a healthy scepticism. This was a wow moment. We took note of where we were and went back to the car and carried on our journey on the island.

When it was getting late in the day, we decided to drive back to the south of the island to go over the bridge to get to the mainland of Scotland. Before we went over the bridge, we stopped at a centre for mementoes. I spotted a book on the shelf showing the history of the Isle of Skye. I flicked through the pages and sure enough an old illustration of Dunvegan Castle was in there and information about the battles there. I read as much as I could until I came across a section on the Marquess of Montrose. He and his men travelled to Dunvegan to fight the McCleod's clan who lived and owned the castle. It all made sense to me then and I showed Steve the entry in the book. We went quiet and it was a eureka moment that what I saw had actually happened. For Steve it was another fact about his past life that he could take home and digest.

LIVING IN TWO WORLDS

22. *They're Back*

Along with my past life recalls, I did home visits to give readings and I continued to see spirit in my house. One Sunday afternoon, I was just settling down in a chair to watch a programme on television, when all of a sudden, a young man in a brown 1970s suit with flared trousers and kipper tie walked into the living room and stood in front of the telly. He looked through me and then turned to walk out of the room again. I was shocked as per usual. I thought it was the lad from before in the same suit. It started to get busy again in our house. The spirit residents must have thought 'she is better now we are able to communicate to her'.

Another time I was in the bath just relaxing when all of a sudden a large woman wearing a pinafore to protect her clothes, she may have come from the 1940s by her hairstyle, she had two small children with her and proceeded to put them in the bath. She stood next to the bath and watched them for a short while. I was just lying still; thinking am I really seeing this. The two children were about three and four years old, sitting where my legs were in the bath. The lady and children then disappeared. It was at that stage I thought am I going mad, I can't have a bath on my own I said laughingly. They were in another time zone and this was like a

191

recording of their life events, and they were doing what they used to do, and time has overlapped to my time. I was flabbergasted that they did not see me as they were not reactive like the monk as he did see me. I told Nat and she said that she felt someone near her when she had a bath too.

I love this house with our spirit visitors and residents. I always say to them, 'I respect you ,you respect us, and we can all live together in harmony'. People who know me think why I say this. It is because they used to live in this house, and it is my home now. I am respectful to them and talk to them when I see them. I have had people come around to do jobs etc and one electrician swore that he had seen someone in the room with him. I said, 'don't worry about it, he won't harm you'. It was the quickest electrical job he did that day and he did not come back!

Another time that spirit made its presence known, to say we are here, was when Nat was staying away for the night, staying at her Nan's house. She told me on previous occasions, that not long after moving into our house, she used to see a man in her bedroom wearing a funny hat with a light on. He walks past her bed as if she is not there, yet she can see him as clear as day. I went into her bedroom to see who he was but I didn't see him so I accepted that she could. She accepted that he was not interacting with her, so it was left at that.

That was until that night she was away, I slept in her room as either Steve was snoring, or I was and thought I would get some peace and quiet. I fell asleep soundly until halfway through the night, I felt I was not alone. I woke up quickly and right in my line of vision, once my eyes adjusted to the dark, was a youngish looking man, fair haired, grubby faced and he was wearing a hard hat with a light on it and his clothes were grubby too. He walked out of the area where an outside wall was, and where an open wardrobe was standing. He then walked past the bed, looking ahead and not seeing me or acknowledging me. He then disappeared into the far wall and that was it. I was stunned but then thought so you are then man Nat sees. He was a miner and his uniform confirmed that. I also felt a sadness with him, like he was walking aimlessly somewhere. I stayed awake in case he came back, but he did not whilst I was awake. I took note of this and thought he is doing what he used to do, or he is stuck.

When Nat came home the next day, I told her that I had seen him in her bedroom. She was happy in the case that I told you so.

After that, every time I went into Nat's bedroom for tidying, or putting her clothes on her bed, I felt the sadness again, and again. All of a sudden as I looked into the space where the miner came from the other night and

I saw him again but only faintly and I felt compelled to talk to him. I asked him what his name was, and he told me. He did not say much but his energy was sad. He then disappeared. I felt him a lot after that but did not see him again.

My curiosity got the better of me and I wanted to find out about the historical part of this area that I live in. I went to the local library and looked at maps and that is when I was given an eye-opening lecture of the history of my area. Apparently, there was a tragedy in 1973 where seven lives were lost. This was a coal mining area amongst other areas where I live in Yorkshire. It seemed that teams of miners had gone down a mine in another area near Leeds, which was their usual duties to dig for coal. These sections of mines can stretch underground for several miles. My understanding is that there are certain places that they can escape from if there was to be a problem with safety. I was told that on this particular day, that men were all along the seam as it's called in the mine spanning across some miles, so there were men underground in my area and dotted across the mine to the other end near Leeds.

The report in the paper said that the men at my end may have disturbed an old Victorian well which they would not have not known about. Either way, the well burst its walls and the men in that area could not escape, it must have caught them by surprise. I have read that men were shouting the others down the line to get out and run to escape. What happened next was tragic. The men near the well didn't stand a chance. They were trapped at the end of the mine and water filled the seam of the mine and it must have been terrifying. This happened at 2.15am, underground, near my house. Word got back about the flood and men were getting out from the other end and some men at the well end escaped but were injured and were helped out from the surface. These men were taken to a local church to be looked after whilst the lives of the seven men trapped were in the balance. Help was on its way to get to them and for days rescue teams went down to recover the men, but due to the water and debris, they were cut off, they could not reach them.

The rescue men which included family members who were miners too, tried their hardest and they were underground for many hours a day, desperate to find them. Eventually, it was deemed dangerous for them to get too close to the area where they believed that the trapped men were. They had to stop the rescue, god only knows how they felt, they had to leave them in the mine. I was shocked and upset by this, but it must have been a very hard decision to come to.

I was told that there was a memorial not far from the spot of the tragedy. I went to see the memorial and there were the names of the men who died. One name jumped out at me; it was the name of the miner who I saw in Nat's bedroom. I was saddened to think that I have seen him and that is why he was sad and the emotion that he gave was strong. It all made sense to me now. They are still down there, and it pulled at me. I could not tell anyone else that I had seen one of the miners as their families may still live near me and that is not right to upset them.

I called on a good friend of mine who is a psychic medium too and I explained what had happened in Nat's bedroom and the miner walking through. He said that the area of the wall where the wardrobe is, has a portal there, which allows spirit and energy to come through. Also, when water flows under a house where an accident has happened, it allows spirit and energy to flow with it, into people's houses and buildings. He said that it needed to be closed as it can be open to anything. So, I decided to close it myself and one day when Nat was away, I spoke to the area of the wall and sent my compassion to the men left behind. I then did my cross over service with the help of Archangel Michael and then once they were crossed over to the other side, I then asked for help to close the portal and then clear the energy in Nat's bedroom. It took a few days for the energy to settle and then we did not see or feel the energy of the miners again. Other than the teenage angst, which is normal, the rest of the room was fine.

Some years later, I attended a memorial for the seven men at a local church, it was the 40th anniversary of the accident. I sat amongst the family and friends of the men. It was a very touching tribute for them and photos of them were shown. Sure enough, my miner friend was there. I sent my thoughts to him as to not make it obvious to the family members. Once the service had finished and people were leaving the service, I then spoke to a man who had sat next to me. He said he knew all of the men as they were his workmates and he escaped. I enquired about the miner whose name I had, he looked at me inquisitively as to say how did I know him. I couldn't tell him the truth, so said I had heard of him nonchalantly. He then explained that the young miner, who for reasons I will call John, John's dad and himself all worked together on the same shift. This man was due to work that day and John was off duty. Since the man had a situation that he had to attend to, at the last minute of the start of the shift, John had kindly agreed to jump in his spot as a favour so they could swap days. The man teared up when telling me that it would have been him instead down there. I felt so sorry for him and I said that things happen and there will always be what ifs. Also, John's dad was in the rescue mission to find the seven men which included his son.

I have had friends come over to my house and they have felt the energy and thought they have seen something move in the corner of their eye. Nat and I accepted this as the norm, but Steve didn't. I was not sure if he believed us until one day, he got the visit he did not bargain for. I went to bed before him that night and he was downstairs locking up the house. All of a sudden, I heard this thundering rush of feet up the stairs. Steve appeared to me in the bedroom and looked startled. I said 'you have seen someone haven't you' laughing. He tried to deny it for man's pride, but he said, 'I saw somebody, and I ran up the stairs'. I believe in "like attracts like "positive energy attracts positive energy and negative energy attracts negative.

We all have arguments and dramas, but I am aware that we have to keep the energy at a positive level as best we can. One night, Steve and I were having a heated 'chat' and the lights in the living room flashed on and off in quick succession. I said 'it's my nan telling you to be good' jokingly. Once we calmed down the light went back to normal. When we have ructions, I say to be careful, my Nan is going to tell you off.

I hear spirit sometimes outside of my ear which is called clairaudience. I have come through the front door from being out all day and I have heard two men talking and having a good chat in the dining room. As soon as the front door shuts, they stop talking. I have heard music before, children laughing and things clattering in the kitchen, my name being called, someone whistling a tune in the kitchen and things turning on and off. This is more so when I am alone.

One time I was making my bed and I knew someone was behind me when all of a sudden, I heard a lovely soft female voice saying, 'David it's time to get up'. I turned around expecting to see the lady and she had gone. Another time in my bedroom I saw a young girl in a Victorian pinafore dress standing in the doorway and looking at me. One night I was stirring from my sleep and I turned over in bed only to be face to face with a young woman standing next to my side of the bed wearing a green dress. In surprise I shouted 'get out my room' because when you are asleep you are vulnerable. I felt awful as soon as I had registered what I had shouted. Steve shot up in bed thinking we had burglars. I didn't mean to shout at her. It took her a while for her to come back again.

LIVING IN TWO WORLDS

23. *Time To Go*

I worked with a lovely girl called Tash, she always had a sunny disposition. One day she confided in me that she was unnerved by some goings on in her new apartment.

She told me candidly that she was in her end suite bathroom attached to her bedroom that morning, when in the mirror she saw somebody behind her. She was so scared, she said she did not like what she had seen and was wary of going into her bedroom without her partner being there. Also, she said that her bedroom light flashes on and off whilst she is in there. I explained to her what I do in the respect of communicating with spirit, and if she wanted me to go to her apartment after work one night. She agreed and seemed hopeful that this situation will be sorted, and it was not her imagination.

Well, the night in question arrived, only Tash and I knew of the reason why I was going to her place, as it was personal to her and she also felt that no one else would believe her. Anyway, I walked in and we sat in her living room just chatting, she also told me the apartments were on the land of the old St George's Hospital which closed down years ago. When all of a sudden, I felt we had company. I got up and told Tash what I had felt, and she looked nervous, poor girl. I got up and said 'Tash, stay in this room and whatever you hear, do not come into the bedroom or talk to me'. She agreed and told me to be careful, bless her!

I walked into the bedroom and sure enough I saw a man in his 40's and the era was possibly about the 1950s. He wore a tweed looking suit, a trilby in his hand, and he sat next to the side of the bed which was Tash's side near the window. I asked him why he was here, and he explained that he was visiting his wife's bedside as she had T. B. (Tuberculosis). I felt so sorry for him, the poor man was still attending to his wife.

As I was talking to him, I noticed a very strong static energy appearing on the other side of the room. I walked across towards the bedroom door and in front of me stood a young lad, possibly about 18 or 19 years of age. He had cuts across his face and was very dishevelled, his clothes were dirty, and he clearly had not much money at the time of his demise. He again would have been around in the 1940's to 1950's. He was so angry, and he was pacing up and down and walked to me and shoved his face into mine. My aura was feeling all of this and I had to protect myself as it was so strong. He was saying things like 'why me', he was aggrieved by something that had happened to him. I spoke to him calmly, to try and get him to tell me what had happened and also to try and calm him down.

He was shouting and was moving around the room aggressively. He then started to bang on the bedroom walls, all across them near me. He was so agitated and worked up, that he was not going to calm down. He stopped momentarily and then started to bang on the walls again, and this time Tash must have heard it too as she shouted to me to see if I was alright. I just said 'Yes, go back into the living room', she quickly did. I said to the lad 'I am trying to help you, what happened to you?'. I said, 'show me, I am able to see it'. All of a sudden, on the wall I was shown a film-like version of what had happened to him. He was what was called a vagrant in those days, someone with no money and nowhere to go.

One evening, he was walking across the road and a car came along and hit him hard and left him lying in the road. The car then drove off and left him there for dead. Luckily another car came by and saw him on the road, picked him up, took him to the hospital and left him there. I told him that I had seen what he projected onto the wall for me, and it should not have happened, especially being left in the road with his injuries. As I spoke to him, he gradually calmed down, and I had the unenviable task of explaining to him that he had indeed died of his injuries in the hospital. He would not believe that he was dead, he would not accept this as he thought he was still in the hospital ward. With this I had to explain that he was stuck in our timeline and not in his era. I told him that when he had died, normally he would have seen a white light in the room or nearby and that was for him to walk towards and then he would cross over to the place that he would find love and compassion, and on the other side of the light, his loved ones would be waiting for him and still are when he is ready. Also, it would be better for him to be in a loving place than being stuck here. He had said that he saw it but was frightened not knowing what it was. I said I would talk him through it when he was ready to go, and not to be frightened of the white light. I started the cross over service and he slowly walked to the light, I recited the Lord's Prayer for him and wished him love and compassion for his journey. He was escorted by his guide and Archangel Michael and then he disappeared.

I collected my thoughts and then went to the man who was visiting his wife. I then explained to him that his wife was not here anymore, she too had passed over already due to her succumbing to her illness. He was just going through the motions of being with his wife when she was ill. I asked him if he wanted to be with her and he said yes. Once again, I did the cross over service with the help of his guides and he confidently walked to the white light and crossed over. I was so relieved for them both. I thanked Archangel Michael for giving them safe passage and for protecting me, also the man's guides to help him. I cleared the old energy from the room and then shut myself down. I then went to see Tash and she said I looked knackered. I agreed that I was, but I was happy that the spirits had moved on. She made me a drink and then I told her who was in her bedroom, then I asked her not to talk about what had happened again. After a while, she then took me home. I saw her the next day at work and she looked a lot happier. She said her bedroom was calm and slept well, and this continued for the future too.

A lot of activity happens here but it has been positive. A few years later Nat and I were stripping the wallpaper off the kitchen walls as we were going to paint the walls and have a new kitchen fitted. I was on the ground and Nat was on the step ladder stripping off the top of the walls. As we were talking, we both noticed that we were not alone. I looked to the left of me and sure enough there was a portly man in solid form, he was wearing a suit with a waistcoat, stood near the back door and then took his pocket watch from his waistcoat, looked at the time on it and then put it back in his pocket and then walked through the back door. When I was looking at him, I had the feeling he may have worked for the railways as he looked like he was setting out to go to work. I looked at Nat and she looked at me and she said, 'Tell me you saw him' and I said I had. I was to see him more after that. He told me years later his name was Bertie. Nat had heard his name too.

I have a bench in front of my house and sometimes I feel the bench go down slightly on the other side of the bench. I say, 'Hello Bertie'" This came to reality one day when my friend came to see me who too is a medium. She said to me 'Who is that man sitting on your bench outside'". I laughed when I realised that she could see him too. I said, 'It's Bertie' She said, 'he is a big man isn't he'. I relayed to her that I feel the bench go down when he sits on it with me. It's funny really because I am aware that he sits there sometimes so I always sit on the other side. A couple of years later, I looked up the residents on the census lists of who lived in my house and sure enough there were tenants from the 1920s and there were young families from the 1940s and Bertie did live in my house between 1940s and 1950s and he actually was a Railway Signaller at a couple of Railway Stations that were near our house and were closed down in 1963.

24. *It's Not What You Think*

One day I tried to teach a work friend how to psychrometrics an item at my house. I got a few things for her to hold to pick up the energy of them and the owner of the item. We were in my dining room where I work spirit wise and it has a sacred space. I asked her what she was picking up from some items and she said that she felt heat and a couple of pictures came into her head. All of a sudden, I noticed her attention was elsewhere. I realised she had seen someone. I asked her what she could see, and she blushed and said that she was not sure if she saw anything. I confirmed to her that she will have done. She then relaxed and said that she had seen a little girl in a pinafore dress from way back in Victorian times. I said that she had seen the girl and I had seen her some years before, and she was relieved at this. I love it when non-believers or people who sit on the fence, see or feel things. It is a shame that if more people were accepting of spirit then they would not deny it or say it's their imagination.

In this house when I sleep, I sometimes leave my body. I normally know when this is happening. I relax and lie down flat on my back. I start to feel a tremor around my body, then I hear like crackling noises or electrical or humming sounds, then if I relax with it then I see flashes of light to the side of me. I feel the pull upwards and I am lifted up above my bed and I can look down and see myself still lying down in bed. I either go to the ceiling or go out of the house and up into the hemisphere. Strange as it sounds, I sometimes see constellations, places I do not know or have been to and also a couple of times I see people where I do not know where they are from nor who they are. I have my thoughts about other beings as I do believe that we are not the only ones in the universe. It is something I keep to myself. Steve has said to me a few times that when I am leaving my body that my body is shaking, and I am going again. It stops me from leaving my body.

There was one time when even I had no control of my body.
Steve and I were on holiday in Tenerife. I love the place and I can relax there quite well. One afternoon we went to a spanish beach oasis park in the capital. It is basically a place where you can sunbathe, away from the beach and the hustle and bustle of the traffic, with a couple of swimming pools, food places and sunbeds for the whole day for a small fee. It is also where the locals go. It was warm that day and Steve decided to go into the pool to cool off. I was on my sunbed chilling out. A while later Steve decided to look over in my direction to see if I was alright as our bags of clothes etc were next to my sunbed. I was keeping watch on them, so he thought. He

happened to look for me and he says to this day, he saw me walk away not far from the sunbed and carry on down a path near the pool. He could not believe that I had left our personal items behind. He swam across the pool and quickly got out, to sprint across to my sunbed to secure our bags. Once he got close to my sunbed, he was stopped in his tracks. I was lying on the sunbed, totally asleep, I had not moved my position since he first left me. He was absolutely shocked. How on earth could I have walked past him whilst he was in the pool, yet be on the sunbed fast out. I woke up and he told me what had happened. I explained that I must have left my body and gone 'walkabout' like I do sometimes. This time though I did not know I went and it was the first time he had seen me do it.

Living in a house that has spirit residents is normal to me. It opens me up sometimes. I do have to ground myself so I am not spacey in the head, or open to spirit not intentionally as this can deplete me of my physical energy as when they come close they use my energy to try and show themselves, manifest, or to communicate with me. If it is not me, they use a power source then they will use electrical items such as lights, they will flicker or blow bulbs, static on the television or anything to use the energy for their purpose.

For many years I have conducted readings in people's homes, but I also had to attend homes where the owner had 'problems' in the house. It ranged from previous tenants not crossed over, loved ones trying to get their attention to suicides and murder victims. Also negative energy of a very low vibration have been resident in some dwellings, due to previous tenants, using a Ouija board or dabbling in something which has opened up a portal, and that allows all manner of energy, spirit and low energy forces to come in because there is no filter with a Ouija board or other rites of calling spirit.

One day I had a phone call on a Sunday dinnertime from a lady who sounded distressed. She had said they are having problems in the house and she was very scared. She asked if I could come around to her house straight away and I did so.

No sooner had I got to the front door, a six-foot man or more was bursting out of the door, his face said it all, he wanted out of the house. He grabbed the two young children and as they were leaving the door to get on the front path. That was when I saw two items being thrown from the top of the stairs with such force, it was a split-second thought to move out of the way. I was bending backwards like the character in the matrix film. They hit the man and he just walked off not looking back. He said, 'it's all yours'. He had gone and I was standing in a doorway thinking ok, this is where others would not go in, but I knew I had to help them as best as I could.

I walked in and said hello to the lady of the house. As we were sitting in the living room, I asked her what had been going on. She proceeded to tell me about the activity in the house when I saw behind her two silver framed photos on a shelf. What caught my eye was that they were both moving and being pushed around like they had no weight to them. I was aware that I could not tell her as I did not want to scare or upset her. I did not see who the photos were of at a distance. I asked her to stay downstairs and leave me alone to see or pick up who is doing this. Bless her, I felt for her as the energy was strong in the house.

As I went up the stairs, I saw a black shadow of a person go across the landing to get away from me. This happens quite a lot as sometimes spirits do not want to be seen or moved over to the other side. I told the black shadow that I could see them, but they stayed hidden. I have this effect on some spirits, but I don't take it personally! I walked into the children's bedroom and straight away I felt the spirit was behind me. I always ask for protection before and during visits. The strange thing was I didn't feel any anger towards me nor the children. I saw in my third eye the children are asleep and then 'he' comes into the room to see them, not in a bad way, just to watch over them. He then started to communicate with me, and he told me that he loved his kids and he wouldn't do anything to hurt them. He was sad and angry at something. I spoke to him and told him that I felt he wouldn't hurt them. I then went into the next bedroom and he followed me and as soon as I went into the room, I felt the energy and static touching my face. It was where a lot of the activity was held.

There were a lot of items and furniture which one particular item was emanating so strongly of a masculine energy, yet I felt the feminine energy too. The spirit man was annoyed in this room in that he felt it was still his family, and family home and said that some items should not be in the room or house. I tried to explain that scaring your family is not the best way to get their attention.

He realised that, and said it was not his intention to do that. He said he loved his kids and misses them. He looked over them at night, and he was not happy about the new man in his house. I explained that he needed to move on to the spirit world as he is stuck here. Spirits do visit family members to check on their wellbeing but then they return to the spirit world. I also told him that loved ones who have passed over will be waiting for him and he doesn't need to be stuck on this earth. He agreed and that is when I performed a crossing over service and invoked his guide and Archangel Michael to help him to go to the light. I recited the Lord's Prayer for a safe journey and sent him blessings and compassion as he didn't realise that his anger was affecting the children. I saw him slowly leave to walk to the light and all of a sudden, he was gone, the room felt light and airy. I then 'cleared' the old energy in the other room and still felt a certain item in the bedroom was carrying a lot of energy.

I went downstairs to see the lady. I told her what had happened and who I communicated with and she agreed that it was her late husband. I explained that he still loves his children and he had visited them at night to watch over them, but for personal reasons he showed his anger to her new partner. I told her about the item in her room and she said it was her new partner's and she will get rid of it. I explained that he had crossed over and it should calm the energy in the house. She was grateful and I also explained that it can take a couple of days or so for the energy to subside and return to normal. I left the house and went home.

A few days later I got an email on my website from the lady's mother and she said the house had calmed down, no more incidents and the couple were arranging their wedding plans. The owner rang me also and she told me that she had thrown the item with the energy out of the house and it feels better in the room. I was glad for the family and her late husband.

Other houses I have visited where previous tenants who still thought it was their home and so after a calm and reassuring chat with the spirit tenants and explained that they had died and needed to cross over to be with their loved ones, then they accepted it. I performed the service with a lot of help from their guides, sometimes their loved ones come forward to help them and of course Archangel Michael.

One house backed off into the local graveyard. The owner was worried in case the visitors were from the graveyard. I went to the back of the house and yard and I did not feel a spirit path from the graveyard to her house. It did turn out it was the previous tenants. I gave the lady some names and her husband pulled out some papers as he recognised a name. The papers were the history of the house and the previous tenants. Sure, enough two of the names were on the papers. I explained that they had not crossed over and as I was talking, I saw the one man walking across the landing to us and the lady said she felt the static. She had said that her little boy sees him on the landing. I had to cross the spirits over as they were man and wife. She said that she did not like going into the outhouse as she feels she is being watched. I went down there and in the corner was a lady from the 1950s era and she was using a mangle and sorting out her wet washing.

The lady owner felt her presence and I explained that she is doing what she used to do in those times. I cleared the energy from the outhouse and property and went home. I always ask people to contact me a few days later to let me know how they are and how the energy in the house is.

One-time Steve came with me to a spirit rescue and he knew to sit away from the homeowner and myself. I was talking to the owner who had said her lights were flashing and there were noises in her kitchen. When we were standing in her kitchen, I saw a lady who used to live there a few years ago. She gave me physical pain to show me what she died of. She had a heart attack and died. The spirit lady meant no harm and she died alone and was not found for a while, so she was stuck on the earth plane. I spoke to her and reassured her that she can move on which she agreed. I explained to the homeowner that I had to be alone to send the lady over. I then conducted the service to cross her over.

Whilst I was talking to the owner in her kitchen, I heard a tinkling sound, it was coming from the living room and Steve was in there. I thought to myself, what is going on! We both went into the room only to see a kiddie's toy like a xylophone being played and the tinkling noise was that. There was no child in the room, certainly not living. Steve was a little alarmed by this. The homeowner said that she hears the toy being played when her son is playing in the room and it is not him, but it does not scare her as she had a child in spirit and accepts that he visits, and he plays with his sibling. I was pleased for her and she was happy for her spirit child to stay in the house. It is not for me to cross the child over if she is happy for him to stay. I left the house and she said the house was better now.

Some house visits I have attended had quite bad energy. Two in particular I remember. A family who were being terrorised by an entity who was getting power from their fear. It was frightening the five-year-old boy when he stayed there. As soon as I got into the house, the dog was growling and looking around the room. I explained to the lady owner that her family needed to stay downstairs. The lady owner stayed in the kitchen with her daughters. I went upstairs for a quick walk around and in the little boy's bedroom, the energy felt prickly and heavy. I went downstairs and told the family 'Do not come upstairs, no matter what you hear!'. I proceeded to go into the little boy's bedroom, and I saw a dark energy form in his room. It was trying to hide, this is when clearing energy from rooms, you must clear inside cupboards, wardrobes etc as the energy can be in there and it seeped into the big cupboard in the wall. I opened the door of the cupboard and said, 'Get out, you don't belong here, you will leave the child alone!'. It rushed out of the cupboard and on to the landing. This was when it was like a stand-off. It put itself near my face making my skin static and I was feeling threatened. I told it that it had to be removed from the house and taken to the place where it belongs. It did not like this at all. I started to recite the Lord's Prayer over and over. It started to growl at me louder and louder. All I could see was this dark energy, no body of a spirit but a very negative energy.

All of a sudden, in the corner of my eye, I could see one of the daughters on the lower steps asking me if I was alright as she heard the growling. I had to turn my head to shout at her quite forcefully to get away, at the time this was the best and only way to get her away to be protected. Thing is when I was being distracted by the daughter, the entity then rushed at me. It was awful, it was powerful, sickening and gave me feelings of despair. I shouted at it to get away from me, as this was a fight I had to win.

It was brooding with energy as I again recited the Lord's Prayer and asked for help and protection from God and Archangel Michael. I needed protection and for this awful energy to go and leave this house to return to from where it came from. I did the service to ask Archangel Michael to come forward and take it to the white light. It felt like an eternity for it to let go of its surroundings without a fight and it left this earth to be dealt with on the other side. It was eerily silent on the landing. I stood there as my whole body was racked with pain and weakness because of the altercation. I collected myself and slowly went downstairs to the awaiting family. I must have looked a sight as I was drip white in the face and they got me a chair. Once I recovered with a drink of water, I had to explain what had happened to a point not to scare them, and to the one daughter why I had to shout at her to get away. She understood that I had to do this, I understood her concern for me, hence her standing on the stairs. I felt shocking, I protect myself every time, but one distraction was a chink in my armour. I left the family and told them that the energy in the house will settle, but I told them not to talk about the entity at all and not to give it credence and energy, 'move on with your lives and do not think or talk about it and you can reassure the little boy for when he stays that it has gone'. I asked them to contact me in a few days.

I went to a church and had to clear myself of any attachments in my aura and from the entity. I always clear my aura before coming home. I was ill for days after as it took it out of me. I learned to never be distracted again. A few days later the owner rang me and said the house is back to normal, the dog has settled, and the little boy loves his bedroom and sleeps better. I was pleased and relieved of this outcome. It was a lesson learnt for me, so I was a little more aware of what can go wrong. After this I had a call to go to a house, in an area which is notorious for spirit happenings in their homes. This may be due to the mining pits in the ground which are now closed but the movement under the ground has disturbed a lot of energy and also if water runs under your house, like a stream or well then this itself carries energy into the area and into the house. As soon as I got to the gate, I knew it was going to be a long night. The owner took me around the house, and I felt the heaviness everywhere.

The owner said that she is leaving the house for good as she cannot live in it anymore. No sooner had she left me alone, I felt the presence of an entity and it was making itself known. I was about to walk into a room when I looked up to the top of the door ledge and there was a bottle of holy water. I thought ok, has she had a priest round? I started to walk down the hallway, and it kept on retreating from me. I just said, 'you are going back to where you came from'! I recited the Lord's Prayer and my heart was racing as this was a strong energy. I then did the service and invoked Archangel Michael to take it away through the white light. This was done soon after. I cleared the whole house of old energy and went downstairs to see the owner, where she made me a cup of tea. Well-deserved, I think.

I told her what I had done, and she said that she was still

leaving the house. I asked her if she had had a priest here at the house, and she said yes but the entity did not go, so he left her a bottle of holy water. I said that at least the next tenants will hopefully have a clear house. She agreed and I asked her to contact me in a few days. She did so and the house was better, and she was still leaving.

25. *Spirit Lessons*

Working with spirit, you learn a lot from them, and I always say we are always learning, from them and about the spirit world. You come across a situation which you realise you will have to be aware of for the next time.

On a lighter note, I went to a man's house where he felt a presence there and he wanted it out. He lived in a lovely area of the countryside. I was sitting in his living room talking to him when a spirit lady stood next to him and she was perturbed. She said that he does not know she is there. I asked the man if his wife had died and he said yes. I explained to him that his wife is still with him in the house. He filled up with tears, he could not believe it. I said that she can hear you and it was her trying to get his attention. I always say to people who have lost loved ones to talk to them by having a conversation with them to let them know you still think of them and love them. I also asked him if he was aware of any water running under his house. He was surprised by this question and he said yes. I asked him if there was a stream under his house and under the opposite houses too where his sister lived, and he said yes, and she is having problems in her house. I explained that spirit and energy travels in all manner of ways including water.

He rang his sister up and told her I was there. She was a bit sceptical, but she allowed me to go to her house. Her house did not have a bad energy, but it did have spirit there. I told her why the energy was there, and she said that the mine nearby closed years ago. These spirit visitors were not staying and not being interactive. She said she will leave them be and is now aware of what it is. I cannot interfere with people's houses if they do not want any help, it is called free will.

I continued to move spirit on from houses and did readings. I also started to give Reflexology to an elderly lady who lived near me. The first time I went to her house, I noticed a man in spirit form but solid sitting on an adjacent seat in her living room just watching on. She was telling me about herself and she was a lovely, funny lady. She then said that she had lost her husband a few years ago and she misses him. I smiled to myself and I thought he misses you too and that is why he sits near her. After a few visits to her house, I decided to tell her of her visitor. I explained that I believed it was her husband just watching over her as she had health issues. She smiled and said that she thinks about him every day, and she was hoping he was near. I explained that they usually visit when we think of our loved ones as we put out the thought of them and they come close. She accepted this and was pleased by the encounter from her husband.

After the end of the Reflexology session, I then gave her

some Spiritual Healing, which in all essence is Hands on Healing. She loved that as my hands warmed her and she also felt comforted by it. I told her when her husband was present also and she said sometimes in bed, she felt a feeling that he was there. I said that if you speak to him then he may come closer and also it lets him know that she knows he is there.

I sat in a spirit circle and a good friend of mine called Pat told me about a film that she had watched, and she felt that I would like it. It originally came out in book form, and then the film came out and is just as informative. It is called 'The Celestine Prophecy', and it was a film that will stay with me for references. I watched it with interest, it was like a 'quest' story, but one part of it rang true to me as I could fully relate to it in my life.

In one scene, a man was in danger as guerrillas were chasing him and they had cornered him up a hill. He had nowhere to go or hide, as he would have been killed when they caught up with him or kidnap him. The man then decided to accept his fate and relaxed, thinking that what happens, will happen. All of a sudden, the guerrillas catch up with him and the man freezes in his spot. He watches them look around for him, he is in plain sight, yet they are looking for him. He cannot understand why they cannot see him, and he holds his breath bewildered by their actions. The guerrillas are shouting to each other in surprise as they cannot understand where he could have vanished.

The man then realised that they cannot see him, he is invisible to them. The guerrillas give up on their search and start to go down the hill and drive off. The man slowly starts to look around and realise they have all gone. He does not understand what had happened, but it made sense to me. Sometimes we can pull in our aura, unintentionally when we are afraid. My understanding is when the aura is very close to our body, then our aura cannot be felt by others. This can sometimes reach to the extent that we are not seen visually either, and that is what happened to me when I was younger with my mother and also the guerrilla with the rifle on the coach in Cairo.

As I have said previously, I don't see events for myself, which is something I am used to now. One day I went to a Mind Body Spirit event which I have been going to for a few years now for the talks and the demonstrations of Mediumship. There was a young Medium giving a talk and the room was packed with people expecting a message from spirit. I sat and listened to all the messages given and I always say that spirit messages go to the loved ones who need it. It was near to the end of the demonstration when the Medium came to me and I thanked him for the message he was about to give me. He said, 'You have lost a baby boy'. No airs or graces to his remark, it was out there for all to hear. I acknowledged that he was correct and said yes. He then said, 'You feel guilty about the loss as if it was your fault', I said yes. I did feel that it was my fault due to me carrying heavy books the day before I lost him, and for leaving him behind as I was in shock! The young medium then said 'You have nothing to feel guilty about, it was out of your hands, he was born stillborn and he was very ill, his intestines had formed on the outside of his body and had you delivered him full term then he would not have survived the birth'. He then continued to say, 'It is better to see this as a blessing so he nor you suffered the consequences'.

I was in tears, a lady next to me looked at me, feeling my pain and was looking at me compassionately. He then went to another person to give a message. My head was spinning, I wish he had told me privately outside of the room and not in front of a full room of strangers. He told me things that I did not know about my son, which I had to take in there and then, though he gave me the answers as to why he died. Of course, I wouldn't have wanted my son to go through the trauma of surviving for a short time, as hard as it was at the time of his premature birth, I was grateful for my message. Thing is, my son has shown himself in spirit to others but not to me, yet I feel his presence from time to time.

I was told later by another medium to put a present for him under my Christmas tree and he will come. Well I heeded her advice and sure enough that Christmas I had my wish. It was the evening of Christmas Day, I was relaxing in my living room, when all of a sudden, I heard loud music coming from the dining room where the

Christmas tree was. I ran into the dining room to see the C.D player being on and playing a record I had not heard in such a long time. No-one was in the room to turn the C.D player on, except my son's presence. I said Hello and Happy Christmas to him, I also told him that I love him and always have. After the track finished, I turned the C.D. Player off. He showed up at Christmas as promised, bless him. One day I will see him, on this earth or when I go home.

I continued to work full time in an Accounts role and in the evenings, I would give psychic and mediumship readings as well as spirit rescues from people's houses. It was one night when my sister rang me and wanted my advice on how to tell our parents that our brother Stephen was very ill with COPD. I was shocked. So, I gave her advice about how to tell our parents about Stephen's ailing health. They too had not spoken to him for some years as they had a fallout with him also. What my Mum and Dad really felt about him was hidden very well.

The next day I decided to ring Stephen's wife and when I asked how he was, she then said that he did not want to speak to me. I was not entirely shocked at that response so I thought I will try again at some time as it would be good to speak or meet up with him to mend our fractious relationship before time runs out. So, I tried to contact him again and once again his wife answered the call and she said that he did not want to know me or talk to me. I was aware that she was looking after him as she was previously a nurse and she was administering his medications etc. I even dreamt that I turned up outside his house to give him a hug and say goodbye to him. This dream was not to come to fruition. After a while of ringing to get to speak to him and refused permission, I then gave up. My sister Maria went to see him a few times but even she had a problem getting to see our brother. Maria did not get on with his newly wedded wife, but she saw her just to see our brother.

About a year later, I got a phone call from Maria to say that Stephen was in a hospice, and his condition was terminal due to the COPD, so he was on oxygen most of the time. Since his wife was previously a nurse, she instructed the hospice to put the D.N.R sign (Do Not Resuscitate) over his bedhead, as she felt that was his wish. I heard about this as my sister felt that it was not his wishes, and also, he could not speak for himself as she did all the talking. I rang the hospice myself and was told that Stephen's wife had instructed them that no family members could speak to him nor visit him. She had told them that it was his wishes so they could not override her. I went ballistic, when I told my sister, she said that she had been texting him and ringing his mobile, but no answer which he would have for Maria.

She went to the hospice one day and actually got through to see him in his room whilst his wife was not there. My sister spoke to Stephen and relayed to him that she was ringing him and was worried as there was no answer and he said that his wife had put his mobile in a drawer, and only she was to answer it. I wanted to turn up at the hospice to see him but then I did not want to put the hospice staff in an awkward position as they are only doing their job and were following instructions.

I kept my head and let it go. I accepted the fact that I will never see him again, and I said aloud one day that I forgave him for all the hurt and damage that he had done to me and the family members who were not around anymore.

About a month or so later, at work, I received the phone call I was dreading. August 24th, 10.00am. I heard my sister crying and trying to tell me that Stephen was dead. My mind was racing, taking it in. I asked her the details and it seems that his wife had taken Stephen away from the hospice and took him home. He had died in his sleep in the morning. You may expect this, but it still shakes you to the core. He was only 48 years old. His wife had told Maria and she said that she was not going to ring around to inform our family. I asked my sister if she had rung our parents and she said that she could not do it and I should do it. She may be the older sister, but it does not matter in these circumstances, it's who is the strongest. I knew my sister could not do it, so that was that. I went to see my manager and had to explain that I had to go home and ring my parents and Stephen's son when all of a sudden word failed me. I broke down. I got myself home in a taxi and the driver did not get any conversation out of me. Steve was at work so I did not disturb him, and I will tell him later.

When I rang my parents and my Dad answered, I had to ask him to get Mum to the phone too and put me on speaker as then both can get the message at the same time. I told my Mum to sit down first, and then I proceeded to give them the news about their only son. The silence was long on the other end of the line. I remember saying I'm sorry that I had to tell them this. My Mum thanked me for ringing them. I knew they were hurting like me and we all had to deal with it in our own way. After a while I rang my nephew and had the unenvious task of telling him about his dad. He was estranged from his dad; he went quiet and thanked me for letting him know. Once again, I said I was sorry about the news. After ringing my parents and then my nephew, I felt like the biggest bitch walking as I was having to give them the bad news.

The reason I have mentioned this is because forgiveness is a hard thing to do especially when the person has died. You cannot go to them and say, 'you hurt me by your actions, but I forgive you'. There is always a feeling of 'If only I sorted this out with them when they were alive' and to say your goodbye's, if that is possible. In this case I tried but to no avail due to his stubbornness or maybe outside events, he could not. I always say to people who have fallen out with loved ones, to try as hard as it is, to see them and make your peace with them before it's too late. My brother has made his thoughts known by communicating through mediums at a couple of demonstrations. He has said sorry for what he had done and also, he was being stubborn for not letting me see him. I have seen him once in my house a few months after he passed. He was standing on my landing whilst I was in the bathroom with the door open, and he was a fully formed apparition. He was young, about in his early twenties, wearing a suit he used to wear when we used to go out drinking in the 1980s. You find that some spirit beings will appear in the guise of their happier times, younger, healthy etc, this is to make you aware that they are well and now exist not in the discomfort that they went with being their mental, physical or emotional struggles. That is comforting and confusing for some people, especially when giving a reading to someone who's loved one was disabled in this life.

26. *Moving On*

Some years ago, I was giving a reading to a lady and her father came through who wanted to speak to her. I started to relay the messages he was giving me, and it was when I said he was standing in front of her, it was when the lady suddenly snapped at me and said 'He can't do that as he was disabled and was in a wheelchair'. I tried to explain to her that in the spirit world he has no physical body so there are no constraints on his health. He is energy and not physical like on this earth. She would not have it that it was her dad. I then said in my head to him, please go to her and give her a sign that this is you as she does not believe me. I felt he was getting concerned that his message was not being taken seriously. Sure, enough she suddenly said out loud, 'Oh my god, someone just stroked my face' and then I smelt tobacco smoke strongly. She then said that she could smell pipe tobacco. I smiled and I said it was Drum, and she looked shocked and said 'yes, it is Drum, as he used to smoke it and I recognise the smell'. It was then that she cried with emotion, knowing it really was her dad trying to communicate with her. I was glad that she understood that her dad was trying to get through to her in any way he could.

I have done quite a few readings for people who have lost their loved ones and they do not know the circumstances of their death. This is a sad part for the recipient as they have to relive the loss of their loved ones all over again with new information. I hope it also helped them with time to know how they passed over.

This normally happens when their loved ones leave the house in the morning and do not come back.

I gave a reading in my home for a mother whose son was killed in circumstances which concerned her. He came into my room and stood beside me, he started to get emotional as his mother was so close to him yet he could not touch her, to comfort her. He then proceeded to show me the film of the event of his death and he talked me through it at the same time. He had died first thing in the morning on a motorway. He was driving his car on a misty morning. His car was stopping and starting and then it stopped in its tracks.He got out of the car and was aware of the oncoming traffic, so he carefully walked around to the back of the car to get to the boot. He opened it and showed me the content of the boot. He then picked up his torch when he told me that it was his Grandad's and he was given it when he died. As he was walking around the car again to look under the bonnet, a car came from nowhere and hit him head on. He was thrown up and away from the traffic, and landed in front of his car on the motorway.

He explained to me that his passing was quick and he did not have time to react. He wanted to comfort his mother and to reiterate that he did not suffer. It was a freak accident and it should not have happened but it did. He expressed his love to her and not to be sad as he is near her always. The mother was understandably upset and I comforted her and explained that he is well in the afterlife and all you need to do is to talk to him, when you need to, he will hear and try to leave signs for her. She left my house, feeling better as she now had the answers to his passing and she accepted it as best as she could, also her son came forward to be with her for a short while.

Other visits from spirit, to explain what happened to them during a reading, was informative but it is hard to see the families go through the heartache again. There was one I cannot talk too much about as it is still being investigated and the other person in the incident is still struggling with the event.

A daughter met her death in a suspicious circumstance, and her friend was present at the time. The family were told that the daughter had taken her own life, yet they could not believe that as the daughter would not have any reason to do that. As I was talking to the family, the daughter came through and she was agitated. I started to pace up and down in their living room. She was upset that her family were incorrectly told by the authorities that she had taken her own life. She had not. She wanted me to tell them that it was by someone else's hands. She then showed me in a film-like vision what had actually happened. It was an accident but it happened with heightened emotion. The family sat and cried, and this mixed with anger and with the verbal knowledge of their gut instinct said that she did not kill herself.

I was asked to ring the police and tell them what I was told and seen by their daughter. I explained that they would not believe my evidence through spirit communication but I will ring all the same and ask them to look into the case again. I also told the family that the other person will speak about what happened but they could not at that particular time as they were too shocked themselves. I said 'The truth will come out, with time'. I sat with the family for a while after the reading and gave them my sympathy and I said 'You know where I am if you need to talk to me'.

The next day I did ring a police phone line and explained that they need to look into the case again. I was greeted with the usual comments but I was anonymous and left the details with them. About a week or so later, I had a phone call from a member of the family, and they told me that they had been to see the other person in the event, and they had told them what really happened. I was relieved for the family yet it was a hollow feeling as this will not bring their daughter back and for the other person whose actions be it accidental, has now got to face the music.

Another thing I have come across is when spirits come through, their personality does not change nor their unique quirkiness, the way they laughed and the way they spoke, but some do express regrets. Many times, I have said to sitters that I am having to repeat what a relative or friend has said, be it straight talking including the odd swear word, which actually gives evidence. I do get a chuckle from the recipient who then says, 'Yes that is them'. Also, another characteristic comes through and that is religion.

I had a lady whose father came through and he was a real character. He showed me what he used to do and in his leisure time. I relayed this to the lady and then as he was talking to me, he then transported me briefly into the pub as a past recall event next to him and I watched him swig back a glass of whisky, whilst standing at the bar and told me he loved betting in the horses. He then said to me 'I would not have believed this, where I am, referring to the afterlife and me talking to you. I thought it was all mumbo jumbo!'. 'I was brought up a Catholic and at the end I was a non-believer, once you died that was it'. He laughed as he was telling me this. I then relayed this back to the daughter once I realised, I was back in the room. She confirmed that he liked his whisky and yes, he did bet on the horses. He was a non-believer and she was pleased he was in a good place.

This was similar to my brother's thoughts. He was a non-believer and for years I used to tell him about the afterlife, especially after my visit there as a child and he knew I saw and spoke to spirit. He didn't believe me though. Then one night I attended a medium's demonstration not far from my house, this took place at least a year or so after Stephen had died. It was a packed room. It was at the end of the session, and I was approached to receive a message. She told me that my brother was with us and he was a non-believer. I said yes and then he said to her "Tell her she was right, it's true, you do go to a better place. It's lovely.". I was glad that he had said that. He then proceeded to tell her that I was a medium too and I should stand next to her and work, she asked me to do as he said. Talk about embarrassment, he was showing me up from the other side.

I then said to her that it's her demonstration and to carry on, she laughed. I then told her that he had a humanist funeral as he did not believe in any religion. I thanked her and went home.

I didn't go to his funeral as I was not 'invited' nor was my family apart from my sister who went. I chose to spend his funeral day in a park in Birmingham which was our childhood park. I sat and remembered our childhood memories, sitting on the grass as it was a sunny day. I saw memories of us playing on the swings and slides and I said to him in my mind, god bless and see you again. I wasn't alone that day, I didn't need to go to a funeral to say my goodbye's.

In my working life, circumstances changed, and I had the opportunity to take redundancy from my job due to cutbacks. This helped me in pushing me to further my life to do the things I should have done years ago. Especially in spirit work and of course writing my book. I also wanted to give talks on subjects of N.D.E, spirit communications, and all manner of paranormal topics to help people who were seeing spirit and coming across changes in their lives that were of a spiritual nature, that they are really seeing and hearing things. Also, their world is changing as people are now awakening to another type of reality.

I remember when I was a child that I thought I was imagining what I saw etc, but it was because I was not told what was going on.

I still feel spirit's presence and get messages from them. I am having to listen to them more, take on what I am being shown and write down what I get. I still get visits from spirit before an event is about to happen or of missing people where it is hard to go to the police as they really do not believe you. There was one such event not long ago where I had no choice but to stick my neck out for the person who was missing as it's not about me.

I was away in Scotland for my birthday, where I watched no television and rested, so I was not aware of a young girl who went missing around that time. When I got back home a week later, I was watching television when an appeal came on for a young girl who had gone missing during a night out. She left her friends behind in a nightclub as she wanted to go home as she had had enough. As the news report was running, I saw the young girl walking up the road and was approached by a man. I saw it in a movie type vision, where they went, what happened to her. It was upsetting as it always is, but I had to take note what I had been shown, so I wrote it all down. I could not get the missing girl out of my thoughts.

When I got the feeling about her again, I went to google maps on my p.c. and went to the area she was last seen. I do not know this area and this part of the country at all. I looked at the road on the screen, when all of a sudden, my eyes shot across the screen as if I was pulled to look and I felt like I was in a car reliving the journey she went on. This went on for a few minutes. I was told by spirit that she is in water. I wrote it all down, and knew it was from spirit and I had to tell someone.

Every day I was hoping that she would be found, and this was to no avail. So, I took it upon myself to ring the police, which in itself you have to prepare yourself for the mistrust and the phone call not being taken seriously. I spoke to a young lady at the local police station to the missing girl. I explained that I have done this before when it came to missing people. I gave her the information, with her being in the water in the area mentioned etc and what I had seen and explained how I work. She listened intently and said she will write it all down and she gave me a case number. She said to leave it to the police and to not get involved. I didn't want to jeopardise their search, but I was involved already. On the news, the story of the missing girl was updated daily but to no avail. So, about a week or so later, I rang again, and told them the details I was shown again and again. I was shown what had happened on that night and spirit was giving me messages that I needed to push the police again.

Once again, I was given a case number and reiterated that she was still in the water as they were moving away from the area as they could not find any clues that she was there. I realised that I had to travel to the area and see and feel what I could, to hopefully help find her. No sooner had I got there I went to the place where she was last seen. I felt a pull and was 'led' by spirit to walk down the road where she lived. Then my legs and my psychic senses took me down roads where I ended up in the area she was in trouble. I knew she was in water and went to an area of water which was in the direction of where I saw on the computer screen. I walked towards the water and saw police frogmen there. They were packing up as they had been searching in the water that morning and in the previous weeks.

I walked alongside the water and I felt she started there but she was somewhere else now, weeks later after her disappearance. I went to walk past one of the frogmen and I said to him, ' She is not here anymore, she started here but she has moved, and she is still in water'. I couldn't believe it fell out of my mouth, and the look on the police frogmen's face was surprised too. I explained that I had rung the station a couple of times and I know it's true.

I walked away thinking they needed to know but they must think I am delusional. As I was walking around the area where she was last seen, I noticed that the police in their van were watching me and where I was going.

They soon left and I carried on walking nearby to another section where I was drawn to. It was a riverbank and I stopped and asked her for help to show me where she was, no mistake, I felt someone hold my hand and pull me down along a riverbank and guided me onto a main road. It was a road I had been shown on the google maps. I said thank you to the person helping me who I believed was her. I then started walking down this main road and felt I was on the right track, but she was further away now. I took note of the road name and I thought I will re-track back to where I came from and get the train home. I felt like I was so close, but I could not get there by walking.

I got on my train and a short while after I started to feel sick with anxiety and then felt a dreaded feeling I get when I know something bad is going to happen. No sooner had I sat with this feeling; the train went over a bridge where a large area of water was. I knew she was there; alarm bells were going off in my head. I did not know the area though. I remembered the train stations before and after this feeling so I could go home and look at a map to try and find the area. I got home later and was overwhelmed by the feeling I had picked up. I sat quietly all night and thought I will look at the map tomorrow. I wrote everything down. It was a long restless night.

The next day, I started to try and find the place on the map between the two stations and I believe I found it. I knew what it was called but it is a very large area. I had to go out and would be back home an hour or two later. I was prepared to ring the police again to say try looking in this area, so when I went back to look at the map of the area where the large area of water was, a newsflash came up on my screen. She was found, thank god I thought, and she can be given back to her family. I was so relieved yet felt so sorry for her and her family that it happened to them. Within the hour it then gave details where she was spotted. She was in the large area of water that I felt ill over. Someone luckily saw her and told the authorities who went out and collected her. It doesn't matter how many times I hear people are missing and then they are found not alive, I still get emotional, compassion is something you need in spirit work, or you will not be able to relate to the loss of someone's loved one.

I went in my dining room and sat in the quiet and I then got a voice saying, 'thank you'. This was followed by a few personal messages and then it went. I wrote it all down and went to ring the police with these messages to pass on to the family but realised that the messages will not get to them and also that the family need their time alone to grieve. I did not get the young girl's spirit back again, but I have kept the messages she left with me. I hope one day she will tell her family these through a medium in the future.

27. *The Time Is Now*

Since the year 2012 came and went, a lot of people have noticed the Paradigm Shift of awareness has happened. A knowing that this world, its people and the environment we live in has changed. We are finding that our tastes in food are disagreeable and, in some cases, we are sensitive to the point of allergies and intolerances. Our network of friends and associates are changing, we find that some people cannot relate to you anymore, and new friends are on the same wavelength. You have your path and they have theirs to follow. Some will catch up with you and some will be left behind in the old thoughts of your life. Also, your type of living may not agree with you anymore either. We are evolving to be the best we can, some living life to the full and be as healthy as possible. We know that there are options for the way we want to live and for our future.

Mindfulness, Meditations and other practices are prevalent due to our previous way of living, which was fast, being stressed and for some "burn-out". We are now aware that we must look after ourselves. There are more Healers, Clairvoyants and Mediums coming to the fore, in a quest for Holistic Healing, also Counsellors and Therapists for trauma. People are taking more time out of

243

their busy lives, where possible, to be in nature, to soak up free energy and recharge their batteries.

Life is hard, no doubt about that but stepping away from the dramas of life, having a few minutes of headspace and looking around you are realising what you have got and not what you haven't, goes a long way. Everyone has a different path in their life, so comparing yourself to someone else's life is futile. They may envy you and you may envy them, but their life may not sit well with you. Some have had bad things happen to them and as you have read about my life so far, it is for me to look for the good and turn life around to live it well.

I do believe that society will change to such a degree in the future between the negative and positive people. I just hope the shift is in positive thinking and actions, as these are greater than negative. That is up to us. I hope that we start to believe in ourselves, that we can use our gifts for ourselves and others. We can walk away from damaging situations and people because you need to listen to yourself and what is best for you and your life. I am not here to lecture but to advise of what is ahead. A spirit guide said to me once in a circle "'You don't own the earth, you are just tenants of it'. How true!

I wanted this last chapter to try and show that we are not alone, our loved ones are near us when we need them. They come when we are in crisis, ill health and when we think of them when we are in need. It is just the case of finding time to feel and be aware of their presence. Signs as I have said before can be white feathers appearing, corner of the eye sightings, and an answer to your question can be relayed on the radio, television and even in someone else's conversation. Also your name being called, ceiling lights flashing, a quick thought about a loved one in spirit and feeling them being close to you. There are so many clues.

We have the ability to use our six senses and they can help you when used wisely. Sceptics of the paranormal are now querying people's stories of incidents, as we are 'opening up' our natural instincts or intuition. This is called the Awakening. A lot of people are aware of things changing in their mind, body and soul. Clearing out their old thoughts and traumas, makes the body lighter. When we are stressed so is the body. I am a grounded person who still has faults, so I am still learning too!
Others are noticing synchronicity events happening for the good and do not know how it happens, I say acknowledge, give thanks and move on.

Children are seeing and using their senses too, signs are given to all of us, we just need to be aware. Do not dismiss what you see or feel, write it down and wait and see. In dreams, they too give an insight and can sometimes foretell events to happen. It's all about keeping the mind open to possibilities. We have free will, so at the end of the day we have to decide what we feel is right and yes, we can get it wrong but that is part of being human. With time we will trust ourselves and what we get and work with it.

To start on your journey, you need to learn about the six senses. Try to practice one at a time so you will then know which sense you can work with and the strength of it compared to the other senses.Some senses come naturally and some take time and practice.

Clairvoyance: Clear seeing, this can be done by clearing your mind of all distractions. This is where you see information in your third eye, sometimes it is like you are watching a film of an event in your mind, flashes, images or it can come through as words. This can before the past, present or future.

Clairsentience: Clear feeling, this is when you feel the information, you may not see the event but you can get a flipping sensation in the stomach, strong palpitations in your physical body and using your gut instinct. Some people feel energy when they walk into a room and feel spirit near them but cannot see them, be it their emotions or illness. This is similar to being empathic.

Clairgustance: Clear tasting, this is getting a taste of something that is not in your mouth.

Clairaudience: Clear hearing, this is when you hear information in the mind and can be in the ears too. It is like telepathic information and you usually hear a voice talking to you as if it is a normal conversation or you can hear music or noises that are not present.

Claircognizance: Clear knowing, this is receiving information that you have no prior knowledge about. It could come in the form of thoughts popping into your mind and this can refer to events that may happen in the future.

Clairalience: Clear smelling, this is to smell odours that are not present in that moment. Some people smell perfume or aftershave, cigarette smoke and even food when spirit is near. This is to let you know that they are close and also to provoke a memory of them.

A suggestion to work with these is to sit quietly for a few minutes, then close your eyes and breathe deeply. Allow your mind to drift off. Be open to what comes into your mind, if you see anything, smell anything, feel anything or hear anything. Take a mental note of anything you get, then when you are ready, open your eyes and write down the sensations you received. If you did not receive any information or feeling at all then don't worry, it all comes with practice.

Also the best way to learn is to attend classes or a workshop on working with your intuition. It is a useful tool to have in your life, especially if you listen to your gut instinct. Sometimes we do not listen to it and it is getting the balance right.

Spirit work should only be done when you are in the right frame of mind and not low in emotion, ill health or just tired. It is a powerful gift and the more you work with it, the more you have to learn, to protect yourself, and to take steps to accept it as a way of life. It is a tool we are all born with and for some they collect more gifts during their life. As you go on your spiritual journey, then sit with learned teachers to do it correctly and safely. Then the world is your adventure.

Enjoy!

Printed in Great Britain
by Amazon

16846937R00145